Negotiation:

How to make deals and
reach agreement in business

Negotiation:

How to make deals and reach agreement in business

Editor
Madan Pillutla
London Business School

Series Editor
Nigel Nicholson
London Business School

FORMAT
PUBLISHING

Negotiation:
How to make deals and reach agreement in business

Published by
Format Publishing
31 Cattle Market Street
Norwich
NR1 3DY

ISBN 1903091322

First published 2004

British Library Cataloguing in Publication data
A CIP record for this book is available
from the British Library

Series Editor
Nigel Nicholson

Editor
Madan Pillutla

Additional editorial and writing
Tom Albrighton, Sarah Powell,
Lin Robinson, Bernadette Sheehan

Cover design
Matthew Knight

Page design
Kaarin Wall

Set in Sabon and MetaPlus

Cover image
Dense shoal of jack mackerel in deep blue sea
by Digital Vision/Getty Images

Page images
Getty Images, except p55 Imagestate

Printed
In the UK by Norwich Colour Print on paper derived
from forests sustained with 'two-for-one' planting

Contents:

How to use this book:

- ☐ Each chapter deals with a broad area of focus, set out in the panel on its first page.

- ☐ Within each chapter are a number of modules dealing with smaller areas of focus. In some cases, modules have 'Read more' links (see below).

- ☐ At the end of each chapter, a 'Looking back' panel summarises the key points.

- ☐ Chapters and modules are listed in the contents. The index lists all topics in alphabetical order.

- ☐ 'Real life' panels present examples and relate them to concepts in the text.

Read more:

- ☐ You can find out more about the ideas and examples in this book by following 'Read more' links.

- ☐ 'Read more' links take the form of a simple title and author reference at the end of the relevant section.

- ☐ To find out more about the work referenced, and (where applicable) buy it online, visit www.formatpublishing.co.uk

Introduction:

by Nigel Nicholson

Negotiation might seem, on the face of it, a specialist topic. It might be for professional negotiators, but it is actually a very general activity within management and the professions – a powerful force for change, effectiveness and value capture in organisations.

In everyday life, in and out of work, negotiation is something we do constantly. It is not always about doing deals over money or resources, it is not always a matter of dispute, and it is not solely the province of salespeople, trade union and management representatives, politicians and peacemakers.

Often the currency is such soft stuff as feelings, obligations, promises and favours; the parties are husbands and wives, parents and children, friends and neighbours; and the outcomes are not just win/lose but various kinds of change. Negotiation is in fact any dialogue where parties aim to reach agreement where interests are divided, actually or potentially. This is the universal process of negotiation – it is intrinsic to social intercourse.

Social life is full of small unwritten contracts that are forged between people who need to get along. In fact, society couldn't function without them.

The core social unit of all cultures is the family. In the circles of kinship people will do favours without expecting return, for the sake of blood ties, but even here brothers and sisters, parents and children are apt to bargain over shares and duties.

Husbands and wives, who mostly have no blood tie to fall back on, have to learn to accommodate each other in everyday divisions of labour and mutual supports, emotional and material. Negotiation is one of the pillars of marriage.

Outside the circle of the family, negotiation becomes even more essential. Our ancestors were faced with the problem: how are you going to deal with the stranger who walks into your camp? The time-honoured human response is to fight or trade. Trading usually makes most sense – see what the other has to offer, and then do a deal.

From these deals come the novel syntheses that build complex societies. True, there are losers, but as this book explains, the best negotiations are those where not only are both parties happy with the deal, but both managed to gain something without evident loss. We shall be looking at all varieties – lose/lose, win/win and win/lose – and what makes some of them collapse and others yield great results for one or both parties.

Effective negotiations are not those that result in the destruction of all opposition, but the ones that achieve outcomes that are more than the sum of their inputs. The greatest organisational achievements are built on the efforts of people coming together and merging interests that looked at first as if they were incompatible. Mergers, major sales, project launches and team building all owe much to inspired negotiation by one or more parties.

But there are some blocks and traps on the way to these outcomes. Among these is the awkward fact that people differ not just in their material interests but also in their style of bargaining. Some people are very hard to do deals with!

First, one has to find a common language. The difficulties can be a matter of culture as much as personality – dialogues of the deaf are liable to occur when people don't take the time and trouble to get on to the same wavelength at the outset.

A key skill here is what I call 'decentring' – the ability to figure out what the world must look like from behind the eyes of the other party. This art is often a key element in a winning negotiation. By helping you to understand how other people negotiate, this book will give you practical power in doing deals.

Reading character and culture is part of this, but also it is important to understand the pressures and demands that your counterpart is subject to. At this point, you might get a nasty shock and discover that the person you are dealing with would really be quite happy to destroy you and take all as the winner, and that she or he is prepared to play dirty to do so. This is where negotiation becomes a contest. Yet even here you can maintain your principles while fending off attacks and getting your own strikes home.

At one level, negotiation is a game. And as in any game, to win you need to make smart moves, anticipate your opponent, know when to play rough and when to make a judicious sacrifice. You need to know when to unleash your killer instinct and when to bow out gracefully, accept defeat and swallow your losses.

Although negotiation is commonplace, strong negotiation skills are not. To negotiate in business, you need to switch into the frame of mind that comprehends the process and its biases.

It is not smart just to drift into deal making on a wing and a prayer, relying on your wits to improvise the best outcome. Your counterparts are likely to be smarter than that. Do likewise. Prepare. Think about your strategy. Consider the opposition and what they might possibly want. Intuitions and spontaneous insights are all very well, but they are no substitute for analytical smartness and thinking in advance.

One cause of difficulty in business is that specific individuals are designated as negotiators, seeming to absolve the rest of us from the need to understand the art of bargaining. 'Every manager a negotiator' should be the motto of the aspiring business. We return to this theme towards the end of this book.

Leaders, line managers and service-providing professionals are all frequently locked into negotiations, whether they recognise them or not. Our view in this book is that they would be much better off if they did recognise them, and did more to prepare for them. No one is more likely to cut a worse deal than the unaware negotiator.

With sound theory and insights from the business world and beyond, this book is here to help you prepare for and approach negotiation in a smarter way, for real business benefit.

1 Overview:

This section covers what negotiation is, when it happens and why negotiation skills are vital in business

What is negotiation?

Negotiation is the process through which two or more parties who are in conflict over outcomes attempt to reach agreement. It is the constructive, positive alternative to haggling or arguing; it is aimed at building an agreement rather than winning a battle.

The situations where negotiation comes into play are often difficult initially, since they involve differences of opinion, but finding a way out of those situations need not be as difficult as it sometimes seems.

In fact, differences of opinion are the starting point for change, development and growth. Provided we can handle them in the right way, they will often open up opportunities for learning and new directions.

When does negotiation happen?

Negotiation tends to be regarded as a formal process that occurs in specific situations. However, negotiation of one kind or another forms part of nearly every business situation, and many situations outside the workplace too. Some examples of business situations that involve negotiation include:

- making **deals** with suppliers, partner businesses or customers

- **internal discussions** between teams and departments within the business over aims, processes and resources

- discussions between **stakeholder groups** within the business (management and unions, for example) over the solutions to specific situations or issues

- **recruiting** new people to the business (interviews and discussions on salaries and terms)

- discussions of **workload and priorities** between managers and staff

- seeking **commitment or investment** for changes within the business.

Whenever you meet a new business contact or colleague, or discuss something new with someone you already know, there will be some sort of negotiation. Even if you only talk about where to have coffee, there is a negotiated transactional exchange going on that will help set the tone and content of the subsequent relationship. In a sense, every business connection or relationship is forged and shaped through negotiation, making skills in this area crucial to success at all levels.

On a personal level, you would use negotiation when buying a used car, agreeing the order in which home improvements will be carried out or deciding which film to see with friends. Although these examples may seem to represent very different domains of social life, the skills required to deal with them are essentially the same.

Why learn negotiation?

Many people believe that the outcomes of negotiations are inevitable – that negotiation is a mechanical process of uncovering the single 'right' or 'fair' outcome. In fact, nothing could be further from the truth. In many situations, there are far more possible outcomes than we might imagine, and our actions have much more impact on which one is realised than we might think. Learning negotiation means we can get to grips with this complexity.

Being a good negotiator brings many benefits, both on an individual level and for businesses. The benefits for individuals include:

- [ ] achieving better **outcomes** from negotiation situations

- [ ] **resolving differences of opinion** without bad feeling

- [ ] creating less fragile, more enduring business **relationships**

- [ ] building an understanding of the **aims, motives and beliefs** that lie behind people's actions

- [ ] **reducing the stress** of negotiations.

For businesses, the benefits of having good negotiators on board include:

- [ ] **reducing costs and overheads** through better deal making

- [ ] avoiding the costs of **failing to make deals** in crucial situations

- [ ] finding **new avenues** for business development

- [ ] creating stronger **alliances** that will withstand change

- [ ] creating a more **positive business culture** in which differences of opinion are welcomed and used for business benefit rather than regarded purely as difficulties to be overcome.

The key negotiation skills

Our 'natural' reactions to differences of opinion can often be very unhelpful. To reach agreement effectively in business, we need to learn new skills and make a conscious effort to use them.

The key skills for negotiators are:

- [ ] creating a **climate** that makes the other party want to engage in negotiation

- [ ] **asking questions:** being a good interviewer; working with, not against, people's characters and values; framing arguments compellingly and putting forward proposals in such a way that people find it easy to choose them

- [ ] **active listening:** genuinely taking on board what the other person says and using it constructively to move negotiations forward

- [ ] **discipline:** preparing carefully, keeping promises and staying committed to your bottom line

- [ ] **flexibility:** being ready to create, consider and evaluate a range of different possible outcomes of negotiation, rather than trying to work towards a predetermined outcome.

About this book

The rest of this book is structured as follows:

- ☐ **chapter 2** looks at building strong foundations for a negotiation: understanding context, goals, outcomes and negotiating styles

- ☐ **chapters 3 and 4** look in detail at the two principal styles of negotiation, co-operative and aggressive: some key techniques for making each style work, and the strengths and potential pitfalls of each

- ☐ **chapter 5** looks at how psychological factors can affect negotiations

- ☐ **chapter 6** looks at getting stalled discussions back on track and closing the deal.

Looking back:

Key ideas from this chapter

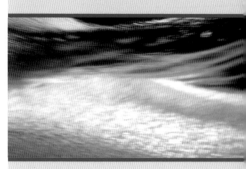

- ☐ Negotiation is the process through which parties who are in conflict over outcomes attempt to reach agreement.

- ☐ Negotiation can happen in any business situation, and in many situations outside the workplace too.

- ☐ Because every business connection or relationship is forged through negotiation of some kind, negotiation skills are vital for decision makers.

2 Preparing to negotiate:

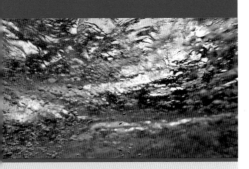

Good preparation leads to good negotiation. This sections focuses on what needs to be considered and put in place before negotiation begins.

Outcomes

An outcome is a possible result of negotiation. Negotiation happens when there is more than one possible outcome from a situation in which two or more parties have an interest, but they have not yet agreed what the outcome will be.

'Natural' negotiating behaviour tends to consist of identifying a preferred outcome ('what you want'), stating it as your goal, and then trying to ensure that it comes about. In this model, negotiation is aimed solely at making your chosen outcome more likely, rather than sharing information with the other party or understanding their aims. If both sides take this approach, the subsequent negotiation will take the form of haggling or arguing. The problems with this 'natural' negotiating process are as follows:

☐ **it produces unwise agreements:** in their desire to secure their desired outcomes, negotiators become overcommitted to them and personally involved with them; the negotiation becomes about saving face, rather than making the best agreement; there is every chance that the resolution will miss the chance to realise many benefits

- **it may not produce any agreement:** a 'natural' bargaining process risks either side walking away in the belief that it simply does not benefit them to reach an agreement – or that the other party simply can't be bargained with

- **it is negative in its focus:** because every move in the game is seen as a concession, compromise or step away from what was hoped for, the negotiation process becomes entirely focused on losses and negatives, rather than what is being gained

- **it is inefficient:** the tendency to start from extreme points of view and work towards compromise means time, effort, commitment and 'emotional capital' are wasted trying to resolve divergent outcomes

- **it is difficult:** the negotiation process itself is likely to be stressful and frustrating, with neither side feeling that progress is being made

- **the relationship is endangered:** the attempt to coerce the other party through force of will makes subsequent dealings more difficult; the side-effects of a fiery negotiation may be long-lasting.

Clearly, approaching a negotiation with a specific outcome in mind can be highly counterproductive. However 'natural' it may feel to us to adopt a position and then defend it, it just doesn't produce the best results.

We need to move beyond the idea of negotiation as being about 'defending our position' and add another dimension to the process. This is the concept of goals.

Goals

Goals are the needs, wants and preferences that we carry with us even before we think about negotiation or the outcomes we want from it – the 'why' behind the 'what'. If outcomes express what we want, or will accept, from a negotiation, goals express why we want it, or why it is acceptable to us.

Outcomes are specific, desired, real-world situations that we hope to bring about through negotiation. They are factual, specific, absolute and often quantifiable. Goals are more fluid. They consist of the business needs that we hope to meet through negotiation. They are often general, subjective and relative.

Goals dictate what outcomes are acceptable. If you adopt a particular outcome and try to achieve it through negotiation, only that outcome is acceptable. Adopting a goal as the aim of negotiation opens up the possibility of other outcomes – but you must know your goals before you can decide which outcomes are acceptable.

To identify goals (whether your own or the other party's), you need to consider a number of factors. 'Hard' or business factors influencing goals include:

- [ ] **strategy:** the high-level or long-term aims of the business

- [ ] **change:** the need or wish to transform the business in specific ways, or to achieve specific outcomes

- [ ] **adaptation:** the need to respond to changes in the business environment to preserve the business's position in the market, or take up a new position

- [ ] **improvement:** lower-level (but still important) aims such as improving efficiency, making savings, improving profit margins or creating better business processes

- [ ] **growth:** increasing turnover; offering new products and services; moving into new areas

- [ ] **projects:** bounded activities directed at achieving a specific outcome.

Goals can also be shaped by 'soft', or cultural factors:

- [ ] **business culture:** the character of the business; they way people relate to each other within it; 'the way we do things around here'; people's perceptions of themselves and the business

- [ ] **an eye on the future:** the need to create or preserve a working relationship that is ready for future deals and has the strength to withstand as-yet-unseen developments

- [ ] **involvement and status:** the desire for the organisation to be treated and regarded as a 'player'; to be visibly influential in negotiations.

Personal factors can also affect goals:

- [ ] **personal pride:** the desire of negotiators to be respected on a personal level; not to lose face

- [ ] **insecurity:** negotiators' own fears of being regarded as a failure, weak, stupid or ineffective

- **peer pressure:** the need to be regarded as a 'good' or 'strong' negotiator by colleagues, regardless of the business benefit of the outcome

- **personal aims:** incentives and motivations (both self-imposed and imposed by the business); career and self-development aims.

Clearly, every negotiation has the potential for a wide range of goals to be involved. But they won't all be equally important. The relative importance of the different goals needs to be considered:

- what is the **primary** or **most important** goal?

- which goals are **subsidiary** or **optional**?

- does the achievement of any goals **imply** or **involve** the achievement of other goals (i.e. if you achieve one, you will by definition have achieved the other)?

- will achieving any goals **enable** the achievement of other goals?

- will achieving any goals **prevent** the achievement of other goals?

Later in this chapter, we will look at setting your bottom line, or minimum expectations. To counterbalance the psychological effect of choosing a bottom line, you also need to focus on an 'aspiration line' – an optimistic outcome for you in this negotiation. If you want a particular result, commit to it now, so you can use it to guide the negotiation process. Deciding on goals and building up commitment to them increases the chances that they will be achieved.

That's not to say that goals should be unrealistic. To be effective, they need to become expectations as well as ambitions, so that when negotiation starts you feel confident that you can achieve them. Your confidence will feed through into what you say and how you act.

Sometimes, the 'real' goal of a negotiation may be completely unrelated to the stated subject, or the 'soft' goals may completely outweigh the 'hard' business goals. The table overleaf shows some fictional examples where the unspoken goal is different from the nominal theme of the discussions to be conducted.

Nominal and underlying themes for negotiations:

Nominal theme	Desired outcome (what is said)	Underlying theme	Goal (what is thought)
☐ Profit from sale of house	☐ *I'm not selling this house for less than £98,000.*	☐ Time-bound financial need	☐ *I need to put the deposit down on my new house quickly. If they offer £93,000, I'll probably have to accept it. I'll find the extra £5,000 somehow.*
☐ Time management	☐ *I can't take on any more responsibilities, there just aren't enough hours in the day.*	☐ Professional standing and self-respect	☐ *I would like to focus on tasks that help raise my status in the organisation and in my profession.*
☐ Working relationship	☐ *I just thought I would drop in for a chat.*	☐ New business	☐ *Have you got any more work for us?*

Three key steps in formulating goals are:

- ☐ think carefully about **what you want** and **why you want it**

- ☐ set **specific** goals that are based on **optimistic and justifiable** targets

- ☐ **build commitment** by writing down your goals and telling someone else about them.

Once you've defined your own goals, you also need to identify the other side's goals, as far as possible. It may involve research – about companies and their markets, individuals and their histories, business cultures and so on. There are many possible sources for useful information, from word of mouth to company literature and the Internet. Time spent on research is likely to bring significant benefits during the negotiation. To understand why the other side is pushing for a particular outcome, you have to know what goals they are trying to bring about. Research can help prepare you for a situation where they are unwilling to share this information with you during a negotiation, or regard doing so as weakening their position.

Read more :

Essentials of Negotiation

by Roy Lewicki, David Saunders and John Minton

Outcomes and goals

To understand the difference between outcomes and goals, let's look at a fictitious example – a price negotiation between a manufacturer and a supplier of raw materials.

The desired outcome for the manufacturer is a reduction in price. The alternative is using another supplier. For the supplier, the desired outcome is to maintain the price at a particular level. The negotiation resulting from the adoption of these two mutually exclusive outcomes is likely to be fairly short and blunt, since there is no room for discussion; it is a 'zero-sum game' (whatever one side wins, the other loses). It is likely that the manufacturer will attempt to coerce the supplier to accept a lower price, particularly if they can show they can pay that price elsewhere and get comparable quality. The discussion will involve implicit or explicit

threats, and is likely to be defensive or openly aggressive in tone.

To avoid going down this road, the two sides need to focus on their goals. On the manufacturer's side, goals might include:

- [ ] the need to **drive down costs** throughout the business

- [ ] the need to achieve a particular **profit margin** on a new product

- [ ] the desire to **build up capital** in order to finance a move into an international market

- [ ] the wish to create an impression of **negotiating 'strength'** to others outside the business (such as shareholders or other suppliers)

- [ ] the negotiator's wish to **'defend' his business** as its loyal servant, or impress superiors with his negotiating skill

- [ ] the wish to **feel like a 'winner'**, not stupid or weak.

The supplier's goals might include:

- [ ] the need to **preserve profit margins**

- [ ] the need to be **competitive** within their market

- [ ] the need to maintain particular levels of **turnover,** or a particular range of clients

- the **need not to be regarded as a 'pushover'** on price

- the wish not to **set a precedent** on price

- the need for the prices they charge to **reflect the quality** of their products as they see it.

The lists could go on and on, particularly for more complex negotiations.

Goals can often be met by more than one outcome. There may be other outcomes, as well as those that are immediately obvious, that will realise goals with less cost to either side than anticipated. Focusing on desired goals rather than desired outcomes allows negotiations to generate new options and solutions by uncovering issues in which both sides have an interest. In this example, they might include:

- the supplier may be in danger of **bankruptcy** if prices are forced any lower; this will ultimately have the effect of reducing competition in the marketplace (which benefits the supplier's competitors, not the manufacturer)

- the supplier may have **information** that could help the manufacturer make savings in other areas; for example, they may be able to make suggestions about how to improve the margins on the product

- the negotiator on the manufacturer's side will **look better** to his superiors if he secures valuable information rather than just concessions on price; securing information will enhance his sense of helping the business to which he is loyal.

This could be just the beginning. Once negotiations focus on the goals that each side wants, the door is opened to finding every deal that is possible in the situation and choosing the optimum one.

It's important to remember, however, that having some goals in common, or agreeing on the goals your solution will meet, doesn't necessarily mean you have achieved total consensus. Shared goals, or diverse goals that can be served by the same outcome, form the basis for a deal between negotiating parties in specific instances. But there will still be many other goals that the parties do not share.

This is an important point to remember in business negotiation. However 'cosy' the relationship between the parties, negotiation should always be aimed primarily at reaching agreement in specific situations.

How many issues?

Negotiations over many issues are fundamentally different from those over one issue. Multi-issue negotiations are more complex, but also offer more potential for trade-offs and flexible solutions. This often makes it easier to find a mutually acceptable solution. For this reason, it can be desirable to turn single-issue negotiations into multi-issue negotiations. The extra complexity is more than offset by the potential to find different solutions.

Before you start to negotiate, consider:

- [ ] what the negotiation is **nominally** about

- [ ] what it's **'really'** about, if different

- [ ] which issues are important for **both sides**

- [ ] which issues are more important (or only important) for **one side**

- [ ] how the various issues **affect each other**

- [ ] whether some issues are **isolated or irrelevant**; whether it would make this negotiation easier to defer or exclude them

- [ ] whether some issues that aren't on the table should be **brought in**, since they might offer the potential for flexibility and different solutions.

If you have control over the number of issues involved in negotiation, give careful thought to which should be included and which excluded. You need to identify your central focus, but have other issues involved to give flexibility and make the process work.

Context

The context of the negotiation can be just as important as the actual content of discussions. Contextual factors can affect one or more of the following aspects of negotiations:

- [ ] **scope:** what issues are included and excluded; what issues can be brought into the discussion

- [ ] **constraints:** the limits to how far discussions can go, or for how long they can proceed; the limits to what can be offered;

how soon opening offers will be made; how quickly a settlement has to be reached

☐ **tone:** the way in which the parties regard each other, or have to be seen to regard each other.

Some general contextual factors to consider include:

☐ **audience:**

 ☐ are the negotiations private or public?
 ☐ what effect will the presence or absence of an audience have on negotiating styles, opening offers, attitudes to compromise and so on?

☐ **time:**

 ☐ is there a deadline for reaching agreement?
 ☐ will any options open up or close down over time?

☐ **cost:**

 ☐ negotiations take time – what will the cost implications be?
 ☐ how will costs increase over time?
 ☐ will other costs be incurred at specific points in the future?

☐ **norms of conduct:**

 ☐ how do people do business in your industry?

 ☐ how do they behave during meetings?
 ☐ what unwritten rules or psychological contracts might affect the negotiation?

☐ **laws:** what laws and regulations affect the negotiation?

☐ **external authorities:**

 ☐ does the deal you make have to be approved or ratified by a third party?
 ☐ what effect might this have on the content of the agreement?

☐ **precedents:**

 ☐ have similar deals been made before?
 ☐ have there been failed attempts to make a deal of this kind before?
 ☐ what are the implications?

☐ **consequences of failure:** what will happen to negotiators on either side, and the businesses to which they belong, if agreement can't be reached?

External standards

External standards provide a guide to whether proposed negotiation outcomes are reasonable. They can be based on factors including:

☐ precedent; records of past agreements

- legislation and regulations

- expert opinion.

Standards are used in negotiations for several reasons:

- to set the direction of negotiation by **restricting** it to a clearly defined number or range of outcomes

- to avoid **wasting time** defending extreme or arbitrary positions

- to assess whether your goals are **realistic** or not

- to demonstrate to the other party that the **outcomes** you want are reasonable

- to appeal to the **other party's sense of what is reasonable and consistent**

- to demonstrate **your** own rationality and consistency, thereby boosting your own credibility as a negotiator and encouraging the other party to follow your lead.

For example, when buying a second-hand car, a used-car magazine listing current market prices could be adopted as an external standard by both sides. The seller would use the listing to decide on a price at which to advertise the car, and the buyer to decide how much he should offer for it. The listing ensures that the goal adopted by the seller is reasonable, not unprecedented and in line with buyers' likely expectations.

However, this is just the starting point. If the car is in poor condition for its age, the buyer may try to negotiate a lower price; similarly, if it has lots of extra features, the seller may use these to increase the price. External standards function as guides; while they indicate the kinds of outcomes that could be acceptable, they don't necessarily dictate the actual outcome.

In some situations the standards chosen by the other party may make it difficult or impossible to reach an outcome that realises your goals. In this instance, rather than attacking the other party's standards, or suggesting that standards are not needed, it may be more helpful to point out the existence of other standards. Alternatively, you can approach a third party who is respected and recognised by both sides to mediate in negotiations. If the negotiation has an audience, their presence or perspective can also serve to impose standards – not necessarily formal – on the negotiation.

One side, many goals

Few negotiations are one-on-one affairs. The more people are involved in a negotiation on each side, the more goals are involved. Every party who gets involved on either side has the potential to bring in new goals, making the 'big picture' harder to keep track of. These additional goals may not necessarily be in harmony with your own, even if people are nominally 'on your side'. How this works depends on how the individuals or groups are involved:

- [ ] they **need to be present** at the negotiation (not necessarily because of their expertise in the subject at hand; perhaps to boost the credibility of the proceedings)

- [ ] they have a direct business or professional **interest** in the outcome of the negotiation

- [ ] they have an interest in the outcome, and their personal **position or status** means that this is important even though they aren't directly involved

- [ ] they have to **approve** or **ratify** the outcome of the negotiation before it can be implemented or followed up

- [ ] they have **differing views** on the outcome that have to be harmonised in the interests of providing a united front to the other party.

The other side may also have interested parties behind the scenes or involved in negotiations. It's worth finding out as much as you can about them, and what they might want from the negotiation. This knowledge can be made to work to your advantage.

However they are related to the negotiation, each party will bring different goals into the equation. Even if their goals are the same as yours, they may have very different perspectives on how the negotiation should be conducted. For the various parties (on both sides), consider:

- [ ] what their **interest** is in the negotiation

- [ ] how they will be **affected** by the outcome

- [ ] how they **can affect** the outcome

- [ ] how you can affect their **position or opinion**

- [ ] whether their **influence is beneficial**; whether you should be trying to increase or reduce it the **links and interdependencies** between the various parties on each side; their relationships and lines of communication, and the implications of these for the negotiation.

As we have seen, the existence of many possible outcomes can be helpful in reaching agreement between two sides. The existence of multiple goals on one side is less likely to be useful, since it diffuses the focus of the negotiation. Different goals need to be in harmony as much as possible, so that if the negotiation achieves its aim, everyone involved is satisfied. If this cannot be achieved, the next best thing is that the outcome of the negotiation should not actively harm anyone's goals.

Know your bottom line

As well as considering your goals and outcomes, it's important to think about the worst deal you will accept: your bottom line. Deciding on your bottom line defines the level below which outcomes would be undesirable or unacceptable.

All negotiators have bottom lines: for a buyer, it would be the highest price he is prepared to pay, and for a seller, the lowest price he is prepared to accept. When these

overlap there is an area of potential agreement known as the 'bargaining zone'; this concept is covered in more detail in chapter 5.

For negotiations that are more complex than simple discussions of price, it may be more difficult to decide on your bottom line. You may have to define it in terms of particular scenarios or particular features of a deal that would not be acceptable to you. In some circumstances, it may not be possible to get a grip on the dividing line between what is and isn't acceptable until negotiations actually start, or until the other side makes an offer. As the other party's goals and desired outcomes become clear, and you relate them to your own goals, you can 'firm up' on your bottom line.

Having a bottom line sets the limits to your flexibility in negotiations. This helps you make a considered response to the other party's suggestions.

Sometimes it is tempting to go with the other party's directions, for a number of reasons:

☐ you want to **make a deal quickly**

☐ you want to seem **reasonable**

☐ you are **uncomfortable** with the negotiation process

☐ you have **little experience** of negotiating.

Having a bottom line is your 'insurance' against any of these dominating your negotiation mindset.

Setting a bottom line is an important step in preparing to negotiate, but problems arise when the bottom line (rather than goals) defines expectations. You need to guard against settling for your bottom line, or least acceptable outcome: the aim of negotiation is to get the best possible outcome. If you use your bottom line as the dominant point of reference, achieving a result above the bottom line may make you feel that you have 'succeeded'. It is far better to define success in terms of how close you are to your goals, rather than how far away you are from your bottom line.

This illustrates why it's vital to have both a goal and a bottom line, defining (however roughly) the range of outcomes that you will accept, from the 'highest' or 'best' to the 'lowest' or 'worst', however such terms are defined. Not having a bottom line opens the door to endless compromises away from your goals, with no sense of where they must end.

Having a bottom line but no goal effectively reduces the negotiation to bargaining over outcomes, since you have only identified a single acceptable outcome. It's not enough to say you will 'try' to improve on the bottom line – you have to decide how much 'more' is realistic and worth aiming for.

Know your BATNA

You need to consider what you will do if negotiations fail; that is, if they cannot produce an outcome that realises your goals. You can do this by identifying and building up your best alternative to a negotiated agreement, or BATNA. Your BATNA is an alternative to reaching an agreement that does not rely on the other party's co-operation. It gives you the knowledge and security that even if negotiations fail, you have something to fall back on.

Having a BATNA gives you options, particularly when things aren't going your way. It means you can:

☐ avoid being **pushed into an agreement** that doesn't serve your interests

- [ ] compare **each possible outcome** that emerges with your BATNA to confirm that a negotiated agreement is better than the alternative

- [ ] know your position if it transpires that the **other party has leverage** (i.e. they don't need you to agree to realise their goals)

- [ ] understand when **you have leverage** (i.e. it will damage the other party's interests if you walk away).

Your BATNA should be as concrete as possible: do plenty of research and establish beyond doubt that it is as workable and desirable as you think. Don't define your BATNA in hazy terms, or just assume you will be able to sort one out if negotiations fail. By doing so, you run the risk of discovering that your BATNA isn't as good as you thought, or even that it isn't a viable option at all.

Read more :

Getting to Yes

by Roger Fisher, William Ury and Bruce Patton

Leverage and threats

The flip side of your BATNA is leverage. If your BATNA embodies what is good for you if you walk away from negotiation, leverage expresses what would be bad for the other party in the same situation. Leverage is the power to reach agreement on your terms; it is based on the threat of a negative outcome for the other party.

In the most basic sense, you can look at who has most leverage in a negotiation through questions such as:

- [ ] whose **need is greater**?

- [ ] who has **most to lose** if a deal is not made?

- [ ] who can **afford to walk away** without reaching agreement?

For example, if you have to travel to a city that is only serviced by one airline, you have little leverage: you need to get to that city at a certain time and for a price you consider reasonable, and the airline knows that you effectively have no choice but to go with them. They have leverage, so they can dictate terms, which probably means that the ticket will be expensive. Although you can choose to withdraw your custom, this won't worry the airline. You don't have leverage

Real life : Celltech resort to their BATNA

In March 2001 Cambridge-based Celltech Group plc, one of Europe's largest biotechnology companies, assigned the marketing rights for CDP 870, a new treatment for rheumatoid arthritis, to the US/Swedish Pharmacia company. The rights were sold for $280 million and 40% of operating profits – the largest such deal ever signed in Europe.

Two years later Pharmacia merged with drug giant Pfizer. Part of the attraction of Pharmacia to Pfizer was the potential of the CDP870 licence agreement. However between 2001 and 2003 market conditions became markedly tougher, and Pfizer signalled that it wanted to renegotiate the Celltech deal. Their goal was to gain a larger slice of eventual operating profits.

Pfizer used their leverage, in the form of the threat that Celltech would have to find a new partner, to put the pressure on. They announced a review of the CDP 870

development programme, and postponed the start of clinical trials. This was a big blow to Celltech, as it would push the planned launch date back from 2006 to 2007. By that time rival products would probably have established a market hold, eroding the market potential and value of CDP870, which had been estimated at over $1.4bn a year. Pfizer's announcement led to a 20% drop in the value of Celltech shares. Doubts were expressed that CDP 870 would ever reach the market. But there were potential consequences for Pfizer too if agreement was not reached: they stood to lose the $60m already paid to Celltech under the agreement.

In the end, an agreement could not be reached. In December 2003, Pfizer gave 90 days' notice of termination of its rights to CDP870. Celltech responded by talking up its BATNA. It emphasised its satisfaction at regaining the rights to CDP870, pointing to the drug's potential value in the treatment of Crohn's disease – a substantial growth market, where CDP870 would be one of the first drugs available. In addition, Celltech could explore further specialist indications which it had been unable to do under the agreement with Pharmacia/Pfizer. What started out as a BATNA had become the strategic direction of the company.

over them; only the market as a whole can provide that.

In business, things may be more complex. It may be that you have leverage in some areas, and the other party has it in others. The more options and issues involved in a negotiation, the more fluid leverage becomes. Shrewd negotiators bring in options and issues that increase the leverage they have over the other party, and decrease the leverage that the other party has over them. To do this, you must know the other party's goals. We saw earlier how personal goals can be just as important as business goals; it follows that leverage can be based just as much on personal factors as on business priorities. For example, the other party's desire to impress others by reaching an agreement gives you leverage, since walking away from a deal frustrates that goal.

However, you need to know about the goal before you can turn it to your advantage. Leverage is often based on perceptions as much as facts; you have the leverage that the other side thinks you have. Deception is a high-risk negotiation strategy, but there may be situations where information needs to be rationed or managed to avoid conceding leverage needlessly.

This illustrates the importance of looking for leverage wherever it can be found. Before negotiation starts, you need to know what leverage the other side is likely to have over you, and what leverage you have over them. People often make the assumption that the most powerful people are the richest, or that the most powerful companies are the biggest. This may be true in the simplest sense, but it doesn't necessarily hold for every negotiation. Look carefully at the issues that are actually on the table to see where the real power lies. You can then change the balance of power in one of two ways:

- ☐ **increasing your choices** so that you need the other party less

- ☐ **reducing their choices** so that they need you more.

In the air travel example above, you could reduce the effect of the airline's leverage by increasing your choices, perhaps by arranging alternative transport at a better price, or by arranging flying to a different city and then travelling on.

Leverage is often unspoken, but you can bring it into the discussions forcefully by making explicit threats. In order for this to be effective, the other party has to believe that:

- ☐ you **genuinely have leverage** (they really will be worse off if you do what you are threatening)

- ☐ the threat is **credible** (you can and will actually do it).

On your side, you need to consider:

- ☐ whether you are **prepared** to carry out the threat

- ☐ what the **consequences** will be for you, the business, the other party and the relationship

- ☐ whether your **BATNA** is good enough to justify playing with such high stakes.

Co-operative negotiators typically let the other party work out what the threats in a situation are, rather than using them as weapons. This plays to the other party's desire to work out the situation and the best way forward for themselves, rather than feeling boxed in.

Aggressive negotiators often use threats explicitly, and openly state what they are prepared to do if they cannot achieve their goals.

Distributive and integrative negotiations

To see how goals, outcomes, BATNAs and threats come into play during a negotiation, we need to understand the difference between distributive and integrative negotiation situations.

In a distributive negotiation, there is no potential for trade-offs on the basis of differing preferences or goals. This occurs when a single issue is at stake. There is no scope for a trade-off; whatever one side gains, the other side loses. Since this is analogous to the situation where two individuals divide a limited resource between them, such as a pie, this is sometimes called a 'fixed pie' negotiation (or 'zero-sum game'). Simple price negotiations, such as haggling in marketplaces, are examples.

Distributive negotiations also occur when there is more than one issue, but each is equally important to the parties, removing the potential for trade-offs.

In an integrative negotiation trade-offs can be made based on the relative importance of different issues to each party. Any business negotiation where there is a range of factors involved has the potential to be an integrative negotiation, because the different parties may in all likelihood value each of these factors differently.

The process of agreeing a price for a house seems at first glance to be distributive. There are two sides in the negotiation. The buyer wants the price as low as possible, the seller wants it as high as possible. With the estate agent's valuation as the starting point, negotiations begin, typically through the procedure of the buyer offering increasing prices until the seller accepts one (or either side gives up and walks away). In fact, as we saw in the section on goals, other factors may come to bear on this negotiation:

☐ the need for the seller to complete the sale within a particular **timescale** (perhaps to obtain money to pay for her new house)

☐ the need for the buyer to **move in** on a particular date (perhaps because of the sale of his own house)

☐ the need for the seller to **move out** on a particular date (into her new house)

☐ the option to vary the **inventory** of the house: reappraise what is included in or excluded from the sale

☐ implications of the findings of the property **survey** carried out on the buyer's behalf

☐ the **BATNA of the seller** (which is probably keeping the house on the market and looking for another seller)

- [ ] the **BATNA of the buyer** (which is probably looking for another house to buy, or perhaps another house that is their second choice)

- [ ] the consequences for, or threats to, either side if they **walk away** from the deal (in terms of money, time, inconvenience or personal factors).

The absence of any of these might also be a powerful factor. For example, if the seller had no need to fit the sale in with another purchase she was making, she would be much less vulnerable to leverage on the issue of timescale.

Clearly, there are potentially more issues to this negotiation than just price. Whether they are used in discussions governs the nature of the negotiation. If information is shared between the parties, and preferences are found to differ, the negotiation can become more integrative. There is the potential for different options to be explored, trade-offs made and a solution reached that satisfies both parties. (There is also the potential for information to be disclosed that changes leverage.)

Win/win and win/lose outcomes

Negotiation outcomes are often characterised as 'win/win' or 'win/lose'. In this simple model, the choice is between both sides doing well, or one side doing well while the other one loses out. There is a tendency to map integrative negotiations on to win/win outcomes and distributive situations on to win/lose outcomes. In fact, in an integrative negotiation, there is the potential for either a win/win or a win/lose outcome.

For example, in the house-selling example, the seller and buyer may come to an agreement that covers factors other than price where both feel they have got a fair deal (that is, one that furthers their respective goals). This would be a win/win outcome to an integrative negotiation. But it may be that once all the options have been explored, the seller uses her leverage or skill to get what she wants in every respect – price, moving date, date of sale and personal convenience. (Perhaps the buyer is so in love with the house that he will accept any deal, and the seller exploits this mercilessly.) This is a win/lose outcome to an integrative negotiation.

What constitutes win/win or win/lose depends on the perspectives of the negotiators. The definition of each reflects the goals, perspectives and opening positions of the negotiators as much as the content of the agreement they reach.

We can't really talk about win/win in connection with 'fixed pie' situations. If two people share a pie equally, neither of them have lost out, but we can't really say that they have both 'won'. However, there is the potential for a win/lose outcome, if one person manages to secure a larger part of the pie. These two possible outcomes are set out in the diagram below, which shows negotiators A and B deciding how much of a fixed pie they will get.

However, adding more factors makes a genuine win/win solution a possibility. If A and B were sharing out a pie, some potatoes and some peas, with A preferring potatoes and B preferring peas, there are many more possible outcomes, some of which are shown in the diagram overleaf.

Two possible outcomes of a distributive negotiation:

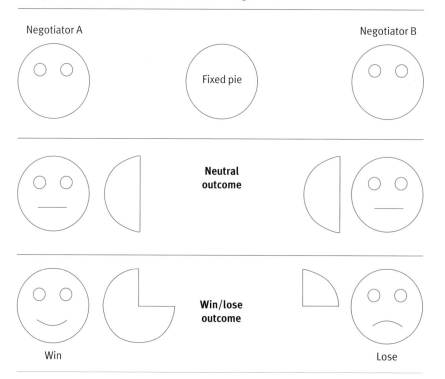

Negotiator A

Fixed pie

Negotiator B

Neutral outcome

Win/lose outcome

Win

Lose

Three possible outcomes of an integrative negotiation:

Negotiator A
Likes pie and potatoes

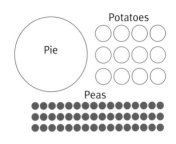

Potatoes

Pie

Peas

Negotiator B
Likes pie and peas

Inefficient but superficially equitable outcome

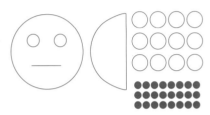
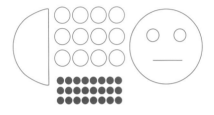

Integrative and equitable (win/win) outcome

Win

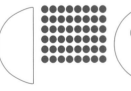

Win

Integrative but inequitable (win/lose) outcome

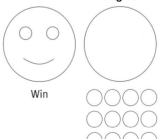

Win

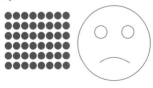

Lose

Firstly, there is the possibility of an **inefficient but equitable** solution where all items are shared equally – a 'fair' outcome, but one that misses out on the win/win alternative. This outcome is likely if the negotiators fall into the trap of 'fixed pie assumptions' (see chapter 5), where their attitudes and beliefs about negotiation lead them to regard any kind of compromise or trade as a form of weakness or 'giving in'.

Secondly, by sharing out the items based on a combination of personal preference where possible (for the potatoes and peas) and equitable treatment or precedent otherwise (for the pie), a **win/win solution** can be reached. Note that this outcome couldn't be achieved without some discussion of the parties' respective goals.

But there is also the potential for a **win/lose outcome**. If A is a hard or aggressive negotiator, with no interest in being fair or building a relationship, and B has no adequate response to these tactics, A might end up with everything he wants – all the pie and all the potatoes. (If he is utterly ruthless, he might negotiate B out of the peas as well, even though he has no use for them, simply to prove his negotiating abilities. This would not be an integrative solution.)

This example demonstrates how the distinction between win/win and win/lose is most useful in getting to grips with the goals on both sides, and the crucial issue of how important the other side's goals are to you. It is this consideration (in conjunction with personal or corporate values) that dictates whether it is worthwhile working towards a win/win outcome.

In some negotiations, such as the recruitment of a new team member, the other side's goals are very important, since they affect your goals. 'Lowballing' by offering the new recruit a very low salary (going for win/lose) is unlikely to boost their motivation, secure their commitment or help your subsequent working relationship. Since all of these problems will ultimately hurt your business as well as the recruit, what looks like win/lose on the surface may end up being lose/lose in the longer term – possibly even worse than not reaching agreement at all. So a win/win outcome should be the aim from the outset in this situation.

However, in another integrative situation, such as the house purchase, each side pursues its own goals. They will make trade-offs, but only with a short-term perspective. As long as their goals

Real life : Making tracks for leverage

The Houston Power & Lighting Company, based in Houston, Texas, was paying the Burlington Northern Santa Fe Railroad $195 million a year to carry coal to their power plant.

The head of purchasing, Janie Mitcham, was unhappy with this on two counts: the price was too high, the service too poor. However, she had little choice in the matter. The railroad had a monopoly on access by train to the plant, and using trains was essential given the large quantities of coal involved. The railroad had leverage over Houston Power & Lighting, and did not listen to Janie's requests for price reduction.

The key to changing the balance of power in negotiations is to change the situation so that the other side needs you more, or – as Janie did – so that you need the other side less. She decided to build ten miles of rail track linking the power plant to the Union Pacific tracks, ten miles away. Burlington did not believe she would do this, as it was a huge project, one that would cost in excess of $24 million, but she went ahead anyway, giving her company a choice of two railroad companies to service the plant. Union Pacific offered a 25% saving over Burlington, and Houston began to save money – $10 million a year initially, and more as time went on.

Janie Mitcham's bold action changed the balance of power with Burlington, but it also ensured that she had leverage over Union Pacific, with the implicit threat of returning to Burlington Northern if their service failed to satisfy. Never again would Houston Power & Lighting find itself on the wrong end of overwhelming leverage.

Read more :

Bargaining for Advantage

by G. Richard Shell

for the deal at hand are realised, either a win/win or a win/lose outcome will do – whatever works. The other side's goals are of interest only insofar as they affect the likelihood of a deal. The two sides will probably not have any dealings after the sale (there are no wider or subsequent outcomes of the negotiation) so only the immediate outcome is relevant.

In a business negotiation, it may not be clear before negotiations start what kind of outcomes are possible. Much will depend on information that transpires during negotiations, opening positions, the attitudes of the other party and your own actions. Aim to establish as early as possible what kinds of outcome are possible from the negotiation, and which is best from your point of view, so you can focus (or refocus) your negotiation accordingly.

Negotiation styles

Goals, bottom lines and BATNAs express the 'what' and 'why' of negotiation. Negotiation style is the 'how'.

Our 'natural' negotiation style is likely to be a function of our own character. If we are naturally confrontational, we will adopt a blunt negotiation approach.

If we are conciliatory by nature, we will tend towards granting concessions in the interests of reaching agreement. Part of becoming a better negotiator is consciously shaping your negotiation style to make it more effective.

Obviously, negotiators are not robots. Our own characters will always shape our negotiation style, and there will be limits on how far we can alter our behaviour. But this doesn't mean we shouldn't try. The difference between what ineffective and effective negotiators can achieve can be considerable.

Management thinker Gerald R. Williams set out to discover the characteristics of effective negotiators. His research focused on attorneys who negotiate legal settlements regularly as part of their work. Williams questioned them on the characteristics of effective negotiators.

Crucially, he did not define what 'effective' meant, since the term means different things to different people – people might approach the same negotiation with very different goals or desired outcomes, and effectiveness is the measure of how successful they are in achieving them.

Objectives and traits of effective co-operative and aggressive negotiators:

	Co-operative	Aggressive
Objectives	1 Conduct yourself ethically 2 Get the best deal 3 Get a fair deal	1 Get the best deal 2 Maximise the benefit for yourself 3 Outdo or outmanoeuvre your opponent
Traits	☐ Trustworthy and ethical ☐ Courteous, tactful and sincere ☐ Fair-minded ☐ Takes up a realistic opening position ☐ Doesn't use threats ☐ Shares information ☐ Explores the opponent's position	☐ Dominating and forceful ☐ Works to a predetermined plan of action, sticks to it rigidly ☐ Does not co-operate ☐ Observes opponent carefully ☐ Takes up unrealistic opening position ☐ Uses threats ☐ Reveals position gradually ☐ Willing to stretch the facts

Williams found that many negotiators (though not all) tended to fall into a particular negotiating pattern – co-operative or aggressive. The results showed that 59% of co-operative negotiators were considered 'effective', compared to 25% of aggressive negotiators.

So neither style had the monopoly on effectiveness, but more of the co-operative negotiators were considered effective. Success depends on how well you work within your style, but it does seem that being co-operative makes it more likely that you will be effective.

The table above (adapted from Williams' findings) shows the objectives and traits of effective negotiators of both types. The implication is that whichever style you choose (or already use), these are the approaches you need to adopt to be effective within it.

Regardless of their negotiating pattern, all effective negotiators are well prepared, observe customs and courtesies, and take satisfaction from using their skills.

The styles in play within a particular negotiation have a profound impact on its tone and the kind of agreement that is likely to be reached:

- **two co-operative negotiators** working together have the best chance of exploring all the options and devising a win/win solution if one is possible

- **two aggressive negotiators** will normally settle into a pattern where each knows the limits of the other's tolerance for their tactics; although there is less co-operation, the outcome is not necessarily worse for either party

- **an aggressive negotiator faced with a co-operative opponent** will escalate his demands until he meets resistance, or the other party has given everything away.

Read more :
Negotiation: Strategies for Mutual Gain
edited by Lavinia Hall

Which style?

Depending on your individual character, you may find it easier to adopt a particular style. If your natural style seems more in tune with the aggressive approach, it might be better to work on improving your effectiveness within this style rather than trying to adopt an approach that is at odds with your own character. The most powerful approach is to use whichever tactics are most appropriate and effective in the situation at hand, whether co-operative or aggressive. Co-operative negotiators sometimes need to 'add some steel' to their negotiation style, while aggressive negotiators can get better results by listening more.

Although the term 'effective' negotiation in the previous section is not rigidly defined, it is confined to the outcome of the negotiation. The focus is on how well negotiators achieve what they want in specific situations, rather than the effects of their actions in a wider sense.

If we broaden our view to include other outcomes from negotiation, such as the tone of the subsequent relationship or the effect on the culture of the business to which the negotiator belongs, we get a slightly different picture of the relative strengths of co-operative and aggressive styles. While either might be effective in specific situations, they have very different consequences if the two sides need to form an ongoing relationship, or if they work together on a daily basis.

Seen in this light, the strength of co-operative negotiation is clear. Its ethical approach and emphasis on sharing information make it ideally suited to forming strong, trusting relationships. The aggressive style, while possibly effective in achieving specific outcomes, may well damage or destroy relationships. A colleague who used them to get what he wanted in the workplace would not be valued as a team player.

Gender differences

Gender is the social difference between men and women. It affects the way people think, the way they act and the way they conduct relationships. Gender characteristics change over time, in line with cultural and societal trends, but many general characteristics seem to be constant. Gender has an important part to play in negotiation, affecting both goals and style.

Men tend to get better outcomes from negotiation than women: although women know as much about negotiation as men, they seem to be prepared to settle for less in many common situations:

- [ ] men **get better deals** on some products (such as cars)

- [ ] women **earn less** than men do for similar jobs

- [ ] women **offer more** in ultimatum situations than men.

This may be because people of different genders simply set themselves different kinds of goals, or it may be due to differences in priorities between the genders.

The following differences in how men and women tend to view themselves may be useful in looking at negotiation styles and goal-setting:

- [ ] men tend to think of themselves as **autonomous entities** ('independent'), while women look at themselves **in relation to their social circle** ('interdependent')

- [ ] men tend to develop behaviour that reflects their own **moral values**; women are more likely to tailor their behaviour to the **needs of significant people** in their lives

- [ ] men's choices are dictated by their **own goals**; women consider their **obligations to and the needs of others** when making choices, and are more likely to consider other people's point of view

- men tend to describe themselves in terms of **power and self-sufficiency,** which they see as important; women tend to consider **likeability or sociability**

- men are less affected by **feedback** than women

- men are happier when they consider themselves to be **better off than others in tangible ways** (such as salary); women are happier when they are **equal to others**

- women are more likely to **disclose their feelings** than men (except when a woman is talking to a man)

- women are better at processing **non-verbal behaviour,** such as body language, than men.

It is important to remember that gender only shapes character in a general way; individuals differ greatly in terms of their approach to negotiation. The points above are intended only as pointers towards the likely negotiation priorities of each gender, or the things that individuals of each gender may need to guard against or tone down when honing their negotiation style. They cannot be used to predict how individuals will behave during negotiations.

> **Read more:**
>
> **Models of the self**
>
> by Susan E. Cross and Laura Madson

Cultural differences

Negotiations between people of different cultural backgrounds can create unique difficulties.

Cultural background consists of economic, social, political and religious context, as well as a shared sense of values and a personal, psychological outlook. Cultural values and norms of behaviour can affect negotiations in a number of ways:

- what business **goals** are considered 'natural' or 'normal'; what kinds of goal it will be assumed that all negotiators have

- what types of **outcome** are considered acceptable

- which outcomes are regarded as **fair**

- what is acceptable **behaviour** during negotiations

- how much **information** needs to be revealed or exchanged during negotiations.

When negotiating, we use fairness standards – cultural 'rules' dictating what is fair and what is unfair – to define what is acceptable. Within cultures, fairness standards can be shaped by social status (class, age, material need), precedent and law. It is crucial to understand that negotiators from different cultures may have different fairness standards.

We can also draw useful distinctions between low-context/high-context, individualist/collective and hierarchical/egalitarian cultures. Where a particular culture falls along each scale can have a big impact on how negotiations proceed.

Low-context cultures rely on a direct exchange of explicit information, with little personal interpretation needed, while high-context cultures prefer indirect communication where context enhances meaning. In a high-context culture, lengthy background information may be required as part of negotiations, whereas in a low-context culture negotiators may be impatient with this. Negotiators need to tailor their approach: confronting problems in a sensitive, indirect manner in a high-context culture, but going for clear and direct negotiations in a low-context culture.

In some cultures, direct confrontation is an effective tool for negotiation, especially individualist cultures such as the United States or the United Kingdom, in which personal achievement is recognised and celebrated. But confrontation may offend a member of a collective society, in which co-operation is part of the social ideology. In some cultures, such as those in China or Vietnam, direct confrontation is associated with loss of face and regarded as being damaging to good relationships. Problems may be highlighted indirectly, in more subtle ways, or even through a third party. Using a directly confrontational approach is unlikely to work in collective cultures.

In hierarchical cultures, such as those of Japan or Malaysia, where people are distinguished in terms of social status, it is inappropriate to confront a person of higher status. Situations of conflict are often dealt with by a social superior. Egalitarian cultures such as the Netherlands or Italy, in which everybody is considered to be more or less equal, would not face such restrictions. Problems can arise when negotiators from such cultures confront or criticise those from hierarchical cultures without realising how sensitive such actions can be.

Collective societies, such as those of Hong Kong or Taiwan, in which obligations to a social group or class are very important, may not be prepared to make staff redundant, while individualist societies, in which personal achievement is rewarded, may regard cutting costs as more important than such concerns.

Of course, these are all very broad generalisations. Not every member of a cultural group acts in exactly the same way. A key part of preparing to negotiate will be to 'do some homework' on the implications of the cultural boundaries across which you will be negotiating. But this information should not be used to try and predict how people will act, only to help you understand why they might be acting in a particular way.

Read more:
Negotiating Globally
by Jeanne M. Brett

Body language

Much of what we communicate is non-verbal: facial expressions, physical movements and tone of voice. In certain circumstances, emotional and non-verbal signals can be highly significant.

People take great care to choose their words carefully, unaware of the other messages they are sending out. Understanding body language can help in negotiations in two ways:

- [ ] you can **gauge how the other party is feeling** more accurately, and perhaps tell when they are withholding information or deceiving you

- [ ] you can **control the non-verbal messages** you send to avoid giving away your own feelings.

Our faces and voices show our emotions most obviously. Facial expressions are often more subtle than we think. It is relatively easy to control them on one level (by forcing a smile, for example), but we often give the game away by displaying fleeting expressions that point to our true feelings. It is generally easier to catch people lying by inconsistencies in their statements. However, where there is a dissonance between words and expressions, expressions win.

Some body language signals and what they can mean:

Body language	Possible meanings
□ Loud and fast speech	□ Anger or fear
□ Soft and low speech	□ Sadness
□ Pausing or 'erming' a lot □ High voice pitch	□ Anger, fear or distress
□ Rubbing, scratching, grooming the body	□ Discomfort □ May indicate lying
□ Crossing of arms	□ Defensiveness
□ Sitting forward	□ Tension □ Attentiveness
□ Sitting back	□ Relaxation □ Indifference
□ Using hands to emphasise points	□ Anger □ Excitement □ Enthusiasm
□ Not using hand gestures at all	□ Caution □ Indifference
□ Smiling	□ Agreement □ Empathy □ Concealing other emotions
□ Eye contact	□ Establishing a bond □ Intimidation
□ Touching	□ Making a point □ Seeking trust □ Building empathy
□ Mirroring the other person's body language	□ Agreement □ Empathy □ Subservience
□ Standing close	□ Establishing a bond □ Intimidation

Body movements are easier for us to control. They are a less integral part of ourselves: we can see most of our own body movements. Still, if not carefully controlled, the body gives us away through micro-gestures: brief and fragmented parts of gestures that point to hidden emotions. An example of a micro-gesture would be clenching the fists while smiling or laughing, indicating suppressed anger.

The accuracy with which we can read body language depends on context. If you already know someone, you will know their habits and be more aware of deviations from their normal body language. It is harder to read the body language of strangers.

The table opposite shows some behaviours that typically occur in negotiations and what they can mean. Which meaning is intended or taken will depend on context and the characters of the negotiators. Some of the meanings are very different, indicating the dangers involved in misreading body language.

Read more :
Telling Lies
by Paul Ekman

Looking back:

Key ideas from this chapter

- [ ] Good preparation is vital to good negotiation.

- [ ] It is important to know the goals you are aiming for, your bottom line and your BATNA.

- [ ] Leverage is what a side has to lose from a failure to agree.

- [ ] Negotiations can be distributive or integrative. Each kind may allow a win/win or a win/lose outcome; the desirability of each depends on your goals.

- [ ] Negotiation styles can be co-operative or aggressive. It is best to work with one that fits well with your character and is appropriate for the situation.

3 Co-operative tactics:

This chapter covers co-operative negotiation tactics: those that focus on building agreement, sharing information and co-operating in the shared interest of reaching agreement.

Firm foundations

A key technique for using co-operative tactics is to stay in touch with everything you've learned and decided on during the preparation stage:

- [ ] all the **issues** involved in the negotiation

- [ ] any relevant **contextual factors**

- [ ] any **external standards** that might be used

- [ ] your **aspirations**: the best deal that you can realistically aim for

- [ ] your **bottom line**: the worst deal that you will accept

- [ ] whether there are **different goals** or priorities on your side of the table, and how you will deal with this

- [ ] what the implicit **threats** are in the situation; what **leverage** (if any) each side has over the other

- [ ] the possible effects of **cultural difference** on the negotiation.

It is worth documenting all these things and keeping them to hand (though perhaps not visible) during negotiations. They will also form a good basis for discussions with colleagues during any time-outs you have during the negotiation. The aim will be to get back in touch with your aims and the means you have of achieving them.

As discussions proceed and information is shared, you will be seeking to ascertain the other party's answers to these points too, and trying to integrate them with your own. If the other party turns out to be a co-operative negotiator too, things should go well. Although your own position will be modified by what they say, they will be prepared to work with your goals as well as their own.

But you also need to be prepared for things turning out to be a little rough. If the other negotiator has no interest in your goals, the relationship between you or even in being reasonable, you need to maintain awareness of the foundations you have built for the negotiation to avoid making unnecessary compromises, hasty concessions or ill-advised commitments. The co-operative approach depends on flexibility, but the limits to that flexibility need to be defined in order to safeguard business interests.

Difficult problems, not difficult people

We often refer to our opponents in negotiation as 'difficult people', but 'difficult' is a relative term that depends on perceptions. In reality, we can all be 'difficult' in any situation where our goals or negotiating style differ from those of others. In fact, those people we regard as 'difficult' are precisely those who are likely to regard us as 'difficult' too. The truth is that it is situations where opinions differ, rather than the people holding those opinions that are difficult. No one can be obstructive in isolation.

Understanding why people are being 'difficult' means focusing on the problem at hand, rather than the people involved in resolving it. The emphasis of co-operative negotiation is expanding or modifying the problem by sharing information in order to make a solution more likely. If this isn't happening, try not to label the other party as 'difficult'. Instead, consider what might lie behind their reluctance to co-operate. It might be one of the following problems:

- □ **lack of common purpose:** not enough groundwork has been done to establish the purpose and focus of negotiations

- □ **lack of ground rules:** the way of working and tone of discussions have not been set, or taken on board by all involved

- □ **lack of experience:** those unused to negotiation may fall prey to 'fixed pie assumptions' or other psychological traps (discussed in chapter 5), even though they sincerely wish to solve the problem co-operatively

- □ **over-emphasis on feelings:** co-operative negotiation depends on sharing information freely, but this needs to be focused on the issue being discussed rather than what people might think or feel about it

- □ **over-emphasis on the past:** information shared must be relevant to the problem at hand, rather than to similar and/or highly emotive events in the past

- □ **over-emphasis on consensus:** co-operative negotiations need to resolve the specific issues on the table, not achieve total alignment of goals or agreement in every area

- □ countering **personal attacks** with personal attacks

- □ **unmet and sometimes unstated expectations:** when the other side believes that you have not met their expectations, it becomes your problem even if you believe that you have, and you will have to address this; on the flip side, you should be very clear about what you expect from the other side

- □ **fusion:** emotional association with particular ideas or positions, or failure to separate the self from the opinions or conduct of others can be unhelpful.

Fusion is normal. We tend to identify with what we own and achieve. It takes a special effort of mind, and often training, to be a good negotiator by cultivating a detached neutrality, in which any displays of emotion are strictly calculated.

Key techniques to overcome these problems are:

- □ getting in touch with others' **personal goals**; separating them from business goals; deciding whether you are in a position to constructively challenge or deal with them to remove them from the frame of the discussion

- **decentring:** aiming to understand the ways in which other people see shared issues; getting 'inside their heads'

- **bringing up all relevant issues:** they can be examined and discussed later on, even if they are challenged at first

- **emphasising** the sense of negotiation as a joint problem-solving task on a shared issue, not a battle between opponents

- **deflecting** attacks by ignoring them or framing them as an attack on the problem

- **defining** people inclusively: reframing from 'you' and 'me' to 'we'

- **involving** the other side by asking for and building on their ideas

- establishing some **constructive ground rules**, for example:
  - no interrupting; each side can speak until their point is made
  - no ultimatums or walk-outs
  - caucuses, suspensions or time-outs whenever requested by either party, however often and of whatever duration required
  - no personal slights, insults or raised voices
  - statements of fact must be backed up with evidence and may not be interpreted as personal remarks
  - suggestions (and challenges to them) must be explicitly linked to the agreed purpose of the negotiation

- ensuring that ground rules will **safeguard the relationships** between those involved while allowing the issues to be examined in a robust and rigorous way

- requesting commitment to a particular **way of working** as a prerequisite for taking part in the negotiation; promptly challenging those who don't adhere to it.

Read more:

The Team That Wasn't

by Suzy Wetlaufer

Listening

Much of your preparation for negotiation focuses on what you will or won't say. When negotiations begin, you also need to focus on what the other party says. This can be difficult when your head is full of your own goals and how you want to achieve them, but it's vital to co-operative negotiating.

Listening has several key benefits, because it allows you to:

- ☐ gauge the **negotiating style** of the other party, and pick up on any particular tactics they've decided to use

- ☐ identify their **goals**, both business and personal

- ☐ infer their **BATNA**.

Basically, listening is the key to fitting your goals and those of the other party together to form an agreement.

Often, we give the impression of listening when we're not. As we saw in chapter 2, the physical signals that say 'I'm listening' are relatively easy to fake, and we often send them even when we're not taking in what people are saying. By simply not talking and looking at the other person's face, we can give an impression of attentiveness, even though we're itching to make our next point. The skill of listening is an active one that needs to be consciously cultivated and carried out during negotiations. The other party may not wish to tell you their goals; they may be revealed in a single word, an aside or even a slip of the tongue. You need to be ready for this by listening to everything they say, not just those parts of the conversation that relate to your own goals. Listening techniques include the following:

- ☐ **keep quiet** both verbally and mentally; don't interrupt; allow the other party to make their points and give them time to sink in

- ☐ **don't be afraid of silence:** remember that negotiations are unlike normal conversations; not every pause has to be filled with a remark

- ☐ **avoid jumping to conclusions:** keep a clear distinction between the divergent/information-gathering and the convergent/deciding phases of discussions

- ☐ guard against **projecting your own expectations** on to others: make sure you hear what they're saying rather than what you thought they might say

- [ ] take time to **examine each remark** made by the other party to identify any new ideas or avenues it might indicate; try not to see everything that is said in terms of your own goals or desired outcomes

- [ ] **seek clarification or request repetition** to ensure you have really heard what is being said

- [ ] consciously use **non-verbal listening signals** such as facing towards the speaker, nodding, making eye contact, leaning forward and making encouraging noises; avoid defensive body language

- [ ] use **agreement** to defuse anger and build empathy (for example, 'I can understand why you feel that way' or 'I'm sure I would do the same'); remember that this does not constitute a concrete concession

- [ ] make **practical arrangements** that will allow you to listen more actively (use a tape recorder rather than taking notes, or ask someone else to take notes)

- [ ] suppress or remove **physical distractions,** such as clocks in plain view or ambient noise.

You may also need to encourage the other party to listen – not by shouting them down, but by behaving in a way that will elicit the behaviours listed above, for example:

- [ ] consistently **exhibit listening behaviours** even in the face of anger (this can set up a reciprocal understanding that the other party should do the same)

- [ ] actively **reject premature conclusions**; stress that the discussion need not reach closure at this stage

- [ ] deliberately **frustrate negative expectations** by responding in a way not foreseen by the other party (not rising to deliberate provocation, perhaps)

- [ ] actively **lift any obligations** that may burden or 'hem in' the other party (for example, 'you don't have to answer now', 'let's return to that topic later', 'you'll need more information before making a commitment').

Space and distance

It can be helpful to preserve a psychological distance or space between you and the other party. Many aggressive tactics (which we will examine in the next chapter) rely on forcing an emotional response. Our instinctive responses come very quickly, while our rational side needs time to make itself heard; the aggressive negotiator knows this, and uses it to advantage. If you respond too hastily, you play into their hands. By focusing on space and distance, you give yourself room to deal with aggressive tactics.

As we have seen, even in a fully co-operative negotiation, it pays to remain 'within yourself' and keep in touch with your own goals. Indeed, this is the foundation for productive, co-operative negotiation. If you allow yourself to be drawn too far into the other person's goals and perceptions, you may not reach the win/win outcome you are seeking. This is one of the pitfalls of co-operative negotiation: taken to the extreme, it can result in too much compromise.

Some good tactics for preserving space and distance include:

- [ ] **pause** before replying; let everything sink in before you speak

- [ ] **take time:** consider answers to daunting or difficult remarks carefully; make sure you understand the situation as it stands fully before you allow it to develop any further

- [ ] **wait:** give the other party time to 'negotiate themselves down' from an extreme position or modify a harsh statement

- [ ] **ask for repetition or clarification:** 'can you just take me through that again?'

- [ ] **paraphrase** what has just been said: 'so in other words…', 'so what you're saying is…'.

- [ ] **take a break:** to avoid fatigue, suggest recesses at appropriate intervals, or even offer to adjourn until a later date; find a reason to leave the room and use the time outside to think

- [ ] request a **caucus** with your colleagues to discuss the position (whether or not you actually use the time for this purpose is up to you).

Many aggressive tactics aim to make the other party feel stupid or inadequate. To deal with this, you may need to let go of the idea that pausing, seeking clarification or asking for repetition makes you look unintelligent, since the aggressive negotiator may be counting on just that.

Negotiations can be intense situations, very different from everyday chats in which much of what is said has no content or motive behind it. It's vital to treat negotiations with care and respect, to make sure you perceive and understand every move in the game as it is made, not afterwards.

Uncover goals and preferences

In co-operative negotiation, the central aim of listening and focusing on the problem is to uncover the goals and preferences of the other party. It's possible that you have some idea of these before negotiation, but it's unlikely that you will understand them fully. Your aim during negotiation is to get them out in the open.

To achieve this, you need the other party to acknowledge and start talking about their goals more honestly, and prevent them from focusing on a particular desired outcome too early. You also need to probe their likely attitudes to different outcomes, but without ever seeming to be pushing them into a corner by favouring one particular outcome.

Uncovering goals is just as important as influencing the other party or bringing them round to your way of thinking, if not more so. Indeed, until you know their goals, you cannot really begin moving them towards particular outcomes, or know how likely it is that particular outcomes will be realisable.

Some good tactics for bringing the other side's goals and preferences into the open include:

- [ ] talking **generally** rather than specifically, to try and elicit information on the other party's strategic goals as well as what they want out of this particular situation

- [ ] making **multiple proposals** and using their responses to establish what their goals and preferred outcomes might be

Real life : Goals and persuasion in Bilbao

The genesis of the Guggenheim Museum in Bilbao shows how very different goals – some on the same 'side' of a negotiation – can be resolved through negotiation and persuasion.

At the start of the 1990s, the Solomon R. Guggenheim Foundation (SRGF) had goals for the future including:

- ☐ generating more revenue

- ☐ realising more value from their collection of modern and contemporary art, of which only 3% could be shown in their existing museums in New York and Venice

- ☐ pleasing sponsors by rotating works through sites in different countries

- ☐ improving the SRGF's international profile.

An attempt had been made to create a museum in Salzburg, Austria, but disagreement between federal, regional and municipal authorities in areas such as environmental impact, allocating funds and the cultural necessity of the project meant that negotiations got bogged down and ultimately failed. The SRGF's director, Thomas Krens, looked to Spain for an alternative site, and adopted

additional goals. He stipulated that the chosen location would need to offer the political unity and finance to make the project viable, plus a site that would allow for the creation of a building that would be an attraction in its own right – an artistic creation.

The authorities of the Basque Country had very different goals:

- ☐ revitalising the local economy

- ☐ building up Bilbao's status as an international city

- ☐ improving the city's image; moving on from times of terrorism and isolationism to become a European and world player.

Negotiations lasted for most of 1991, but in December an agreement was signed that paved the way for work to begin. The foundation stone of the new building, designed by American architect Frank Gehry, was laid in October 1993, and the museum opened in 1997.

In contrast to the SRGF, with its relatively homogeneous set of goals, the Basque authorities had to deal with different opinions among political groups, citizens and the media about the merits of creating a Guggenheim museum in Bilbao – before and after the deal was made.

Some saw the project as cosmetic, or wasteful of funds. Others thought that too much power over local affairs was going to Americans, or that they were dictating every aspect of the deal.

The proposal had to be seen in the context of Bilbao's ambitious programme of regeneration. Other projects, such as improving the city's port and airport, building a metropolitan railway and creating a new conference centre could be regarded as boosting the economy more directly. The task of the authorities was to harmonise these differing views by persuading people that the project was worthwhile, and a sound investment in the future rather than an indulgence.

- [ ] probing the **goals** behind their desired outcome: 'why do you say that?'

- [ ] probing their **attitudes** to win/win and win/lose: 'how would that benefit us both?', 'how would that help me?', 'what would I get out of this deal?'

- [ ] suggesting **alternatives**: 'what if we were to … ?', 'how would you respond if we … ?'

- [ ] requesting **advice**: 'what would you do if you were me?', 'how do you suggest we move ahead?', 'how have you dealt with situations like this in the past?'

Try to make all questions as open-ended as possible, to get the other party talking about their goals. Questions that can be answered 'yes' or 'no' may tend to stall discussions, or lead them to a dead-end. To keep things moving along, go for 'what' or 'why' questions that don't allow yes/no responses.

Generating options

Having identified the goals of both sides, the next step is to create or uncover outcomes that realise them both. It's unlikely (although possible) that any outcome will realise all goals of both sides completely; the aim should therefore be to find the outcome that gets closest to this. The key characteristics of this phase are:

- [ ] **openness:** sharing information on why different outcomes are better or worse

- [ ] **flexibility:** keeping options open on both sides and being open to the options proposed by others

- [ ] **choice:** providing choices to the other party and staying in touch with your own choices.

Choice is the touchstone of co-operative negotiation. People do not want to feel that they have been coerced into agreement, that they have no choice, or that there is only one option. They want to feel that they have made the right choice from a range of options. At every turn, choice should be maximised. No one should feel closed down, boxed in, pressured or coerced.

This approach can seem counter-intuitive in situations where you want to 'close down' the negotiation as quickly as possible, perhaps because you need to find a solution quickly. Remember the other party is almost certain to feel this as a pressure and resist it. People often need time to gather information to support a decision or reassure themselves that they've chosen the right option, even after it is clear that they have settled on a particular course of action.

Some pointers for generating options are:

- [ ] **be flexible:** keep every possible avenue open for as long as possible, even if it is becoming clear (to you) that some are unrealistic

- [ ] **create a 'branching' discussion:** aim for the discussion to be constantly widened out, not narrowed down, with new options and alternatives being generated or invented wherever possible

- [ ] **brainstorm:** throw many different ideas out without criticism or analysis; ensure everyone understands that the aim is to generate options, not choose a solution; move into a process of consideration once this is complete

- [ ] **develop common purpose:** create a sense of working together on a problem; build a consensus on the issues facing everyone

- [ ] **create futures:** ask 'what if' questions to explore different scenarios for the future, emphasising that there is a choice to be made about how things work out

- [ ] **take perspectives:** demonstrate your own willingness to look at the issues from the other side's point of view; actively encourage them to look at the issues from your point of view; build outward from areas of agreement to explore areas of differing perspective

- [ ] **adapt and re-use:** if the other party makes a suggestion that doesn't meet your goals, aim to reframe what they have said, rather than flatly reject it; emphasise that you agree with it in principle but need to refine the details

- **agree with your opponent:** you can agree with many things that the other party says without necessarily conceding anything concrete; this will disarm anger, build empathy, create a sense of shared problems and enhance your credibility as someone who understands

- **appeal to ego:** aim to integrate suggestions the other party makes into the solution wherever possible; people don't reject their own ideas and this approach will make you seem more reasonable and intelligent to them

- **promote choice:** remember that the other party wants to feel they are making choices, not being coerced; offer them an alternative whenever you can, and repeatedly emphasise that they have choices

- **allow choice:** as a possible solution emerges, focus on making it easy for the other side to choose it rather than forcing it upon them; provide reasons why they should go for it; emphasise the fact that it meets both sides' goals; continue to emphasise the other choices available (while perhaps pointing out that they don't meet everyone's goals).

Building a common reality

At the heart of many conflicts where each side blames the other are differences in perspective. The situation is the same for both parties, but they have differing views of who is responsible for problems and how they should be put right. Bringing these perceptions closer to create an agreed, shared picture of what is going on can help to resolve such situations.

This can be achieved either through an intermediary or directly. If the relationship has deteriorated seriously or discussions have broken down, some kind of outside help is likely to be beneficial, if only to ensure that the correct process is followed or simply to discourage the parties from walking out again.

The table opposite shows how the differing perceptions of a sales team and a product design team from the same (fictional) company who are in conflict might be brought together, pointing the way forward to constructive changes.

The perceptions thrown up by this type of exercise may be surprising to both sides. The key is to identify common goals – the aims shared by both sides. This is the starting point for building up a picture of reality on which both sides can agree.

Building a common reality:

Sales say	Product Design say	Agreed version	Action
☐ We talk to customers so we know what they want. Product Design should listen to what we say and respect it more.	☐ We're got more experience in this industry and don't like being ordered around by salesmen.	☐ Sales are the interface with the customer and are responsible for passing on what they hear effectively.	☐ The process of passing on customer feedback needs to be as transparent as possible, to minimise perceptions of information being misused.
☐ We never get what we ask for. It's infuriating and makes us look stupid to customers.	☐ Their requests aren't thought through properly, so we have to change them.	☐ There have been failures of communication, with both sides at fault at different times.	☐ Development processes need to be changed to improve communication and highlight potential problems early on.
☐ They don't understand the pressures we face.	☐ Just because we don't bring in revenue directly, no one listens to us.	☐ Support from Product Design is crucial to Sales; involvement is crucial to Product Design.	☐ Cross-department teams, 'shadowing' and other methods could help each team understand the other's concerns.
☐ We try to make the relationship work – they are the problem.	☐ They're arrogant, obsessed with figures and know nothing about design.	☐ Sales have not yet found the appropriate tone for their dealings with Product Design, and vice versa. This has resulted in false perceptions on both sides.	☐ Both sides need to consider if any of their actions might have given rise to the other's perceptions, and think of different approaches that will change them.
☐ They've got no idea about real business – what do they do all day anyway?	☐ We try to make the relationship work – they are the problem.		

The departments in the example have a shared goal in getting well-designed products to as wide a market as possible. They need to keep this in mind in all their dealings. Within this, the actions identified will help them realise shared aims including:

- [ ] **focusing on customers** and using their feedback to improve

- [ ] creating processes that help both groups to **work together** more effectively

- [ ] building a strong working **relationship** and creating a **pleasant working environment** (as well as 'getting the job done')

- [ ] understanding the processes, priorities and pressures of **other teams.**

The key to the success of this method is that the parties do not give up anything concrete – they simply concede that things might be described differently. This prepares them for changes that won't be regarded as concessions, but improvements for mutual benefit.

> **Read more:**
>
> **Overcoming Group Warfare**
>
> by Robert R. Blake and Jane S. Mouton

Persuasion

The adage says, 'only negotiate from a position of power', but often that's impossible. There will be times when the other party has leverage, but you still have to negotiate. One example of this is a discussion between a business that wishes to increase its prices and a client that it cannot afford to lose. In this kind of situation, skills in persuasion are vital – they allow us to achieve outcomes we want in situations where we cannot command or control others.

We sometimes speak as if the ability to persuade is a talent, and that people either have it or they don't. But those who persuade well base their power on consistent, observable principles. Basically, they know how to appeal to particular human desires and needs in a compelling manner. By learning how they do so, we can become more persuasive too.

Psychologist Robert B. Cialdini has identified six fundamental principles of persuasion. They are based on decades of behavioural research into what makes some people better at persuading than others.

The table opposite lists the six principles of persuasion, along with

Six principles of persuasion:

Principle	Basis	How to use it
Liking ☐ People like those who like them, and are more likely to follow their suggestions.	☐ Similarities between people in terms of views, preferences and perceptions make them like each other.	☐ Find something you share with the other party and talk about it. ☐ Find something you like about the other party and mention it.
Reciprocity ☐ People repay in kind.	☐ If you give something away, however small or intangible, people will feel that they 'owe' you something.	☐ Give concessions in the areas where you hope to receive them. ☐ Exhibit desirable behaviours to elicit them from the other party. ☐ Share information to get information.
Social proof ☐ People follow the lead of others who are similar.	☐ People look to those around them for cues on how to behave; peers give the most powerful cues.	☐ Try to build commitment among the peer group of the person you are trying to persuade. ☐ Think about where they look for advice or guidance and how you can use it to your advantage.
Consistency ☐ People align with their clear commitments.	☐ Once people have made a public or explicit commitment, they tend to stick to it as they want to appear consistent.	☐ Seek written confirmation of everything that is agreed. ☐ Consider how audiences for negotiations might usefully reinforce commitments.
Authority ☐ People defer to experts.	☐ People are more likely to accept a suggestion if it is backed up by authority.	☐ Make sure the other party knows the depth of your experience and knowledge. Don't assume they already know.
Scarcity ☐ People want more of what they have less of.	☐ The less available something is, the more people will want it.	☐ Highlight unique benefits to the outcomes you can offer, or exclusive information you are revealing during negotiations.

the basis for each one and suggestions for how they can be used.

These principles aren't 'tricks', or even individual techniques as such. They shouldn't be used in isolation or in sequence, but as part of a consistent, rounded approach to co-operative negotiation. They are organising concepts for the general approaches listed in this chapter as applicable to situations of uneven power.

Co-operative persuasion is built on the idea that the strongest agreements are created when people 'persuade themselves' by choosing, of their own free will, options that have been put before them framed in a particular way, rather than being tricked or coerced. People do not resist their own ideas.

Read more:

Influence

by Robert B. Cialdini

The pitfalls of co-operation

If used effectively, co-operative negotiation techniques have the power to create agreements that meet the goals of both parties and forge long-lasting relationships. Using such techniques can also help to create a more pleasant, less stressful negotiating environment. However, co-operation isn't a guarantee of success or harmony. It also has the potential to be used ineffectively, and may even damage business relationships. The potential pitfalls for co-operative negotiators are:

- ☐ failing to see the difference between (unnecessary) **concessions** and (necessary) **co-operation**

- ☐ being too **trusting**; expecting the other side to play by the same rules

- ☐ being overly **tolerant** or forgiving of aggressive tactics; trying to bring aggressive negotiators round to a more reasonable approach

- ☐ **giving in too easily** to aggressive tactics, and (as a result) reinforcing the belief that they will be effective again in the future (this can have very negative long-term effects for the business)

- ☐ linking **personal emotions** too closely with the negotiation; wanting to be liked by the opponent; trying to appeal to emotions (guilt or compassion) to force agreement.

Possible results of these are:

- [ ] too much **unnecessary compromise** or concession

- [ ] too much concern for the **other party's goals,** over your own

- [ ] an **inappropriate tone;** one that is 'too friendly' or unbusinesslike

- [ ] too much emphasis on the **discussions** themselves, and not enough on getting the right outcome

- [ ] too much emphasis on the **relationship** between the parties, and not enough on the deal at hand.

There is also the critical issue of what happens when a co-operative negotiator meets an aggressive one. If not used carefully and knowledgeably, co-operative techniques may result in the negotiator being 'steamrollered' by an aggressive negotiator. For this reason, it is vital to be familiar with aggressive tactics, even if you don't plan to use them. You must be able to recognise them and deal with them. The next chapter will help.

Looking back:

Key ideas from this chapter

- [ ] Co-operative tactics focus on listening, uncovering goals and sharing information.

- [ ] Co-operation is founded on the principle that it is only problems, rather than people, that are difficult.

- [ ] The key to using co-operative tactics effectively is to work with the other party as a team, while keeping sight of your own goals.

- [ ] Co-operative negotiations proceed through questioning, sharing information and exploring options, until the best way to meet both sides' goals is identified.

- [ ] Co-operative techniques can be ineffective or damaging if taken to extremes.

4 Aggressive tactics:

This section deals with aggressive negotiation tactics: when you might use them, how you can deal with them if they are used on you, and how to avoid using them where a co-operative approach might work better.

Ultimatums

Giving an ultimatum threatens the other party with a breakdown in discussions if a particular course of action is not agreed. It means saying things like 'take it or leave it', 'this is my final offer' or 'sign now or the deal's off' in an aggressive way.

Ultimatums present a choice or threat that is already present in a situation and intensify it by making it immediate. The aggression stems from the removal of the opportunity to consider the position or discuss things further – the negotiation is forced towards closure.

If you are issued with an ultimatum, you have several options:

☐ **dismantle the threat:** attempt to bring the negotiation 'back from the brink' and open up discussions again by highlighting the many options that are still present in the situation

☐ **question the threat:** ask why the ultimatum is being delivered now, or what pressures are making it important to reach agreement at this time

☐ **call the bluff:** refuse to agree and see if the other party will really carry out the threat (whether this is feasible or not depends on your BATNA)

- **agree:** give in completely and concede whatever is demanded.

Looking at these options highlights why using ultimatums is a high-risk strategy. It's a real all-or-nothing gamble. The possible responses range from total agreement to total refusal. You might get a reasonable response, but if that's what you are seeking, you are better off simply acting reasonably. You should only use ultimatums if you are happy with the other party either agreeing completely or just walking away. It's hard to imagine many business situations where this might be the case; they are likely to be characterised by overwhelming leverage on your side, coupled with total indifference to any subsequent relationship.

Do try to avoid using ultimatums yourself as they usually lead to negative emotions. If you feel you have to use them, do so as a last resort and only if you are willing to follow through. Usually, it is better to use softer tactics such as pointing our your alternatives.

You may also wish to point out to the other party that they have a choice, and talk through the consequences of each choice. Or there may be a need to highlight the necessity to reach agreement within a particular timeframe.

Anger

In many ways, resorting to anger is the precise opposite of using the principles of persuasion listed in chapter 3.

By showing anger, you risk:

- not being **liked**
- setting up an **unwelcome reciprocity** (i.e. the other party feels justified in anger)
- failing to elicit **willing commitments**
- reducing your own **authority**.

Anger will not persuade anyone to do anything of their own free will. It *might* force agreement, but the other party's opinions will remain unchanged – except that they may fear, dislike or despise you more than they did before. So while it may secure a particular outcome, the price is high in terms of the subsequent relationship and the tactic itself is a high-risk one.

The negotiator who uses anger may be hoping that you respond in kind. If they are more in control of their emotions, they may be able to embroil you in argument, then pick their way through the wreckage, taking what they need while you recover your poise.

It is almost never constructive to respond to anger with anger. Instead, take time and space to defuse it and find out what's behind it. Having acknowledged that anger may be justified, and perhaps taken a time-out to let it cool down, you can try to unpack the reasons for it. This will uncover a goal that may have been hidden – very likely a personal one. Or, if the storm quickly disperses, you may suspect that the anger was not genuine, but simply a tactic aimed at reducing your emotional resilience.

Good cop, bad cop

This technique uses contrasting negotiating styles in a cynical way to elicit agreement. Two negotiators are used. The 'bad cop' puts pressure on the other party through aggression, threats, explicit leverage and anything else that occurs to them. It does not have to be done in a careful way, or even be based on the realities of the situation, as long as the other party does not walk away. Any demands made are an emotional device. There is no intention to make the other party agree to them. There may not even be any concrete demands made, only a sustained aggressive assault.

Once the shake-up is complete, the 'good cop' takes over. By appearing more co-operative and reasonable, this second negotiator capitalises on the gratitude of the beleaguered negotiator by offering a 'way out' – the outcome that both the 'cops' really want. The 'good cop' typically offers some information that the 'bad cop' allegedly doesn't have, or dismisses the other's demands as ludicrous in order to make his own seem reasonable and well-founded. Essentially, the antics of the 'bad cop' are intended to throw the persuasion credentials (see chapter 3) of the 'good cop' into stark relief.

The first step in responding to this tactic is to recognise it. Just by stating that you have recognised it, you may well bring it to a halt. The second is to dissociate any emotions evoked by the situation from the facts of the case. Neither of the negotiators is your friend, and in any case, you are here to resolve a business issue, not make friends. The negotiation needs to be refocused on the issue at hand, with all parties agreeing to discuss them in a reasoned way. If that fails, you could try requesting to deal with just the 'bad cop' and attempting to reach an agreement with him. If nothing else, this will disrupt the 'script' of the tactic.

Inertia

Inertia is simply not responding during discussions – stonewalling. The technique is similar to pausing before replying, but it is taken to an extreme so that the other party feels uncomfortable.

Inertia gives the impression of dissatisfaction without anything concrete being articulated. A written record of the meeting will show nothing. However, the effect is highly disconcerting. In fact, the effect of silence can be so powerful that people 'fill the space' by 'negotiating themselves down'.

Using, or responding to, inertia is a question of degree: how long can silence continue before it becomes an aggressive tactic? As we saw in the previous chapter, not responding for a while is often a good way to deal with an unexpected or unwelcome move from the other party. If you are faced with inertia repeatedly, or in response to trivial remarks, it is being used as a tactic rather than as a way to preserve time and space. Be aware of it and guard against modifying what you have just said; perhaps offer the other party a break for deliberation, rather than just sitting there. This shows that you have spotted the tactic.

Consistency traps

Consistency traps are the aggressive flip-side of the principle of consistency, one of the principles of strong persuasion that we saw in chapter 3. The first step in setting a consistency trap is to get the other party to commit to a particular standard (perhaps an external one) or principle in general terms. The aggressive negotiator then springs the trap by shifting the focus to a specific area and invoking the same standard, demanding agreement on the grounds that to do otherwise would be inconsistent. This approach appeals to people's natural desire to seem consistent.

An example would be the consultant who negotiates a price for a difficult job that is then used as a basis for pricing a succession of more basic jobs.

The key to responding to consistency traps is stepping out of the trap before it closes. You need to be aware when negotiators are putting leading questions to you, and try not to answer them too quickly or without thought. Try to get more information to clarify why the question is being asked; skirt around the trap before stepping in.

If you do get caught, you have two choices: accept the implications of the trap or risk losing face by admitting you are being inconsistent. Factors such as the audience for the negotiation may dictate the effect this will have. In many situations, it may be that losing face is preferable to accepting the implications of the trap.

Read more:
Influence
by Robert B. Cialdini

Information and deception

Aggressive negotiators aren't afraid to use – or abuse – information to get what they want. This can include tactics such as:

- ☐ **bending the truth** slightly

- ☐ **withholding** information

- ☐ **exaggerating** facts that support a particular outcome

- ☐ **playing down** unhelpful information or denigrating its source

- ☐ being **economical with the truth;** giving partial or misleading answers to key questions or failing to reveal details that are obviously relevant or important to the discussion

- ☐ using a **flood of information,** perhaps of a technical or complex nature, to drown the other party in details they don't understand

- ☐ using **surprise** by bringing new factors into the discussion unexpectedly

- ☐ **feigning confusion:** pretending not to understand what has been agreed when the time comes to close the deal; 'forgetting' important information that has transpired during the negotiation

- ☐ **deception:** introducing false information into the discussion.

All these are in contrast with the co-operative style, which depends on the honest and open disclosure and sharing of information. All information should be seen as a weapon by negotiators. The co-operative negotiator uses this 'weapon' in a neutral way, as a team resource, only withholding information when there is a good reason to do so. However, the aggressive negotiator is more likely to be deliberately deceptive.

Information tactics have two functions: using information (or the absence of it) to influence the outcome directly, and withholding or giving it in such a way as to affect the other party on an emotional level, by creating feelings of confusion, disorientation, dismay or simply the desire to get the negotiation over with.

The responses have been covered in the previous chapter: requesting clarification or repetition, taking time to process new information and making sure you understand it before discussions proceed. These offer protection against tactics based on revealing information in particular ways; there is little protection against barefaced lying.

Along with anger, the abuse of information is one of the highest-risk negotiation tactics there is. If you use such tactics, you jeopardise the negotiation process itself and also the relationship between the parties. The stronger the tactic used, the graver the violation of principles such as reciprocity, social proof and consistency; the results will be unpredictable and almost certainly negative. You need to be absolutely sure that the consequences of using them are better than the consequences of not using them. Typically, this will be in situations where you will have no dealings whatsoever with the other party outside the negotiation (the

working environment of the confidence-trick operator).

However, as with all aggressive tactics, it's a question of degree. Bending the truth is often accepted as part of negotiation; when it transpires later that this has happened, the other party may not want to 'rock the boat' by raising the matter. But barefaced lying to secure an agreement is unlikely to go unchallenged. The relative power of each party, the tone of their relationship, their respective negotiating styles, the audience and cultural norms will dictate what is and isn't acceptable.

Distraction

Distraction tactics aim to disorientate the other party by allowing peripheral events to disrupt the proceedings, for example:

☐ **answering phone calls** during discussions

☐ allowing **people not involved in discussions** to enter the room; breaking off to talk to them

☐ **leaving the room** unexpectedly; not returning for a long interval

☐ **physical activities** indicating lack of attention (such as fiddling

Real life : Aggressive negotiation

In July 2004, retail magnate Philip Green's proposed takeover bid for Marks and Spencer was withdrawn following weeks of intense and often heated discussion. Green, owner of UK retail chains including BHS and TopShop, presented himself to shareholders as the natural choice to turn round the ailing retail giant, while newly appointed chief executive Stuart Rose, also hugely experienced, maintained that his 'back to basics' style business plan was the way forward.

The proposal was nominally friendly, but was pursued in an uncompromising way, reflecting Green's direct personal style. The story highlights some problems with the aggressive style (and some that can affect all negotiators):

☐ **use of information:** market rumours leaked out before Green was ready to announce his bid, depriving him of the weapon of surprise and giving M&S time to prepare a response

☐ **unrealistic opening offers:** the leaked information saw M&S shares rise in value, making Green's opening offer look unrealistically low (he initially offered 290p–310p per share, eventually increasing the bid to 400p; just after his bid was withdrawn, Goldman Sachs valued shares at 416p)

☐ problems with persuading from the **principle of liking:** Green's forceful personal style probably didn't enhance his standing with shareholders in a traditional, long-established company like M&S

- problems with persuading from the **principle of authority:**
  - M&S's appointment of Stuart Rose as chief executive meant that Green could not recruit his old ally and deprived him of a potentially powerful collaborator
  - the bid's financial backers (from Merrill Lynch and HBOS) and proposed non-executive directors seemed reticent in supporting the bid
  - a former chairman of M&S was known to back the cause, but did not do so publicly
  - Green's failed bid for M&S in 2000 did nothing to boost his credibility as a serious contender in 2004
- **managing the context (external authorities):** the City's Takeover Panel, asked by M&S to set a cut-off date, intervened earlier than expected; this forced Green to make his final offer before all the details of M&S's plans were known
- **failing to use leverage:**
  - the deficit in the M&S pension fund was a 'hot issue' that could have been used to Green's advantage, but he failed to capitalise on this potential source of leverage early enough in his campaign to turn it to his advantage
  - different goals on the M&S side (a third of shareholders were in favour of the takeover) could have been more effectively exploited, perhaps through a less aggressive approach
- **unwise ultimatums:** to satisfy his backers, Green needed to be recommended by the M&S board; he pushed discussions to the brink by threatening to walk away if this didn't happen (but withdrew before receiving a response)
- **one side, many goals:** the Green consortium seemed to have internal tensions; Goldman Sachs, a financial backer, seemed uncertain, perhaps mindful of their reputation.

None of this means that aggressive negotiation can't be effective in some circumstances. But if aggressive negotiators misjudge the level of aggression that a situation will bear, they can put the pressure on themselves rather than their opponents.

Philip Green's huge success in other areas bears witness to his business acumen. With his existing retail chains taking on M&S in the high street with renewed vigour, it remains to be seen whether the both sides' BATNAs will be better for their fortunes than a deal would have been.

with things on one's desk, using a computer and so on)

- [ ] **body language** indicating boredom (such as ostentatiously looking at clocks or watches, staring out of the window and so on).

As tactics, these are high-risk in terms of the relationship and blunt in terms of their effect. They can only serve to undermine the other party and the negotiation itself; it's unlikely that they will further your goals. They could conceivably be useful when it has become clear that the negotiation cannot meet your goals and you wish it to break down, but the co-operative approach of terminating the discussion in a professional way is better.

If you think these tactics are being used on you, simply call the other party's bluff: offer to reschedule the meeting at a more convenient time.

Giving up

Sometimes aggressive negotiators will walk out of a meeting, either as the follow-up to an ultimatum or unexpectedly. The aims of this tactic are:

- [ ] to unilaterally **seize power** over proceedings (which are halted until both parties are back at the table) and demand concessions before they can continue

- [ ] to **shock** the other party into agreeing to particular demands or closing a deal quickly

- [ ] to **emphasise** the importance of particular issues (through the timing of the walk-out) – perhaps those that have not been given enough weight by the other party

- [ ] to register **protest** at the negotiation style or tactics of the other party.

As with other aggressive tactics, before you walk out you need to be sure that the effect of doing so really is going to be better for you than staying put. You also need to be prepared for your bluff to be called, and the other party to allow discussions to end on this note. Whether this happens depends on leverage – who has most to lose. You could get off your high horse and return to the table, but this reveals your tactic for what it is. And if you ever do it again (or do it repeatedly), it will quickly lose effect and your credibility will take a nosedive.

The pitfalls of aggression

We've already seen how the wider contextual effects of aggressive negotiation can pose dangers to your relationship with the other party, or your reputation. It also brings several pitfalls in terms of the negotiation itself:

☐ allowing the desire to **dominate the opponent** to distract from goals

☐ allowing **ego** to distract from goals

☐ failing to force agreement through **inappropriate or ineffective** use of confrontation, ultimatums or bluffing

☐ becoming **over-reliant on aggressive tactics** that have worked in the past; using them so often that they become ineffective or start to look ridiculous

☐ misjudging the **level of aggression** that the negotiation can sustain

☐ **alienating the other party** through hostility or intolerance.

Using aggressive tactics is a question of degree and judgement. They may well be effective in moderation; the choice to use them depends on the character of the negotiator.

Looking back:
Key ideas from this chapter

☐ Aggressive tactics are based on coercion, forcing emotional responses and the tactical use of information.

☐ They have their place, but often involve a degree of risk and need to be used with great care.

☐ Co-operative negotiators need to understand aggressive tactics so that they can respond to them.

5 Negotiation psychology:

Our perceptions and beliefs can have a profound effect on all aspects of negotiation. This chapter looks at some of the ways in which this happens.

The bargaining zone

In a 'fixed pie' or distributive negotiation, there is typically a 'bargaining zone', or range of values that both sides will accept. If we return to the house-purchase example in chapter 2, we can see what this means in practice.

For the sake of clarity, we will exclude any other factors that might make this a integrative negotiation and focus solely on price. This means we can define the bargaining zone mathematically. There is still a bargaining zone in integrative negotiations, in terms of a range of mutually acceptable outcomes, but it is harder to define or delineate.

Suppose the seller wants £100,000 for the house, and the buyer offers £90,000. It may be that the seller would in fact settle for anything over £93,000, and the buyer would go as high as £95,000. Together, they have a 'positive bargaining zone' stretching from £93,000 to £95,000. This is shown on the diagram opposite.

The bargaining zone defines the outcomes that are acceptable to both parties. However, there are degrees of acceptability: lower prices will be more attractive to the buyer, and higher prices more attractive to the seller. Once an

A positive bargaining zone:

offer is made within the zone, it is possible that the seller will accept it, the probability of this being determined by how near it is to the upper end of the bargaining zone.

In a 'fixed pie' negotiation, the opening bid will often be outside the bargaining zone, but not so far outside that it seems unreasonable. For example, the buyer might make £90,000 his opening offer, expecting to have to revise it upwards, but he would not start at £50,000.

In house sales, if the seller does not like the buyer's offer, they sometimes make a counter-offer, or (more often) simply reject the offer and wait for a better one from whoever bids next. A simple rejection probably indicates that the offer was outside the bargaining zone, but supplies no information

about how far it was from the start of the zone. In fact, until a bid is accepted, neither party can be sure there is a positive bargaining zone at all, unless they discuss it.

This is what makes estate agents' valuations useful: they provide a reference point from which constructive negotiations can begin – assuming both parties agree with the valuation. When two people haggle, the opening bids are extreme (way outside the bargaining zone), and the bargaining zone itself is very wide. Buyer and seller converge on it gradually through a process of offer and counter-offer.

The endowment effect

The endowment effect is the tendency we have to overvalue what we already own. Ownership constitutes a very strong framing effect on negotiations. We will start from a much higher valuation of something if we already own it. It is easy to see how this can cause problems in business negotiations, for example when discussing the sale of a business.

We can see this clearly in the house-purchase example, and anyone who has been in this situation will recognise the phenomenon. While we regard our own houses as deserving the full valuation, if not more, we would be unlikely to offer to buy a similar house for a comparable amount.

Third-party assessments of value can be very useful, and an awareness of the endowment effect can help prepare us for the situation when buyers and third parties agree on a value of something we own that is far lower than our own estimate (as is likely to happen).

Framing effects

Frames are mental structures we put around situations, issues or decisions in order to make sense of them. In negotiation, frames consist of issues such as:

- [ ] what **information** is included, and what is ignored

- [ ] which **options** are considered, and which are 'off the radar'

- [ ] which **goals** are considered reasonable

- [ ] which **bottom lines** are considered realistic

- [ ] which **BATNAs** are created, perceived or understood

- [ ] what **opening offer** might be reasonable.

Negotiation frames provide the point from which 'gains' or 'losses' will be assessed in a relative sense. They 'anchor' the negotiation process at a particular point (a price, say) or in a particular area (one kind of possible deal, say).

This can be useful where the starting point is drawn from an objective standard of some kind, since it prevents negotiations wasting time in totally inappropriate areas. Problems arise when 'anchors' are chosen on the basis of scant information or even instinct, and negotiators begin from diverse or divergent positions, making agreement more difficult.

This illustrates why offers to 'split the difference' (accept an outcome midway between two divergent positions) can be treacherous. The offer seems equitable, but the points defining the 'difference' to be split might be completely arbitrary. The process of negotiation itself can cloud the origins of anchor points in our minds, making us feel that we are 'getting somewhere' even though we have started from completely the wrong place.

In an unfamiliar situation, or one where we don't have a lot of information, we cling to anything that seems concrete or definite, even when we've made it up ourselves. We may also look to historical precedent, or other negotiation situations, to find our anchors; what we find may not always be appropriate or helpful.

Gains and losses

One very important consequence of our need to frame negotiation is the way we perceive negotiation developments in a relative sense: that is, whether we feel we are 'gaining' or 'losing' with each step.

This is important because we have different attitudes towards 'gains' and 'losses'. We can see this in action if we return to the house-sale example, but look at a situation where there is a *negative* bargaining zone. Let's say the buyer will go as high as £92,000, but the seller won't settle for less than £98,000. There is no positive bargaining zone, but perhaps they discuss the option for them to 'split the difference' and go for £95,000.

Framing effects mean that the way in which this price is presented to them – or the way that they regard it – has an impact on how likely they are to accept it. If the seller regards it as a 'loss' of £3,000 from her 'final offer', and the buyer regards it as spending 'another' £3,000 on top of his 'final offer', they will be more inclined to walk away. The seller risks not selling the house for a while, the buyer risks not finding another house. But they might regard these BATNAs as better than 'losing money'.

However, the same situation can be framed differently. The seller might regard the price as a 'gain' of £3,000 on top of the buyer's final offer; the buyer might regard it as a 'saving' on the seller's 'final offer' of £98,000. Again, nothing has really been gained or saved; the same sum

How framing effects can make the same outcome look like a gain or a loss:

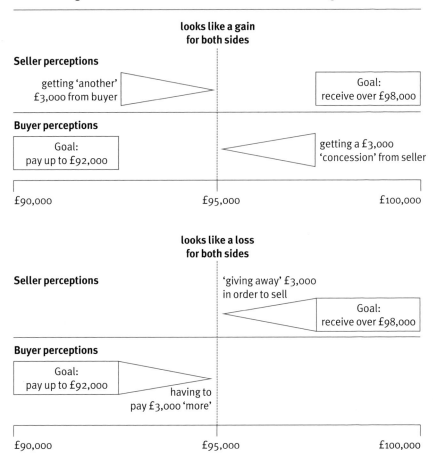

**looks like a gain
for both sides**

Seller perceptions

getting 'another'
£3,000 from buyer

Goal:
receive over £98,000

Buyer perceptions

Goal:
pay up to £92,000

getting a £3,000
'concession' from seller

£90,000   £95,000   £100,000

**looks like a loss
for both sides**

Seller perceptions

'giving away' £3,000
in order to sell

Goal:
receive over £98,000

Buyer perceptions

Goal:
pay up to £92,000

having to
pay £3,000 'more'

£90,000   £95,000   £100,000

of money is going to change hands. The diagram above shows the same situation framed both ways.

In reality, nothing concrete has been gained or lost; it is our anchors that create 'gains' and 'losses'. As we have seen, different anchors would create a positive bargaining zone, with no need for any 'concessions'.

Read more:

Choices, Values and Frames

edited by Daniel Kahneman
and Amos Tversky

Prospect theory

Prospect theory states that we evaluate gains and losses from a neutral reference point, and that our attitudes towards outcomes are greatly affected by whether we regard them as 'gains' or 'losses'. We react to the threat of loss with an aversion stronger than our desire for gain, even if the gain and loss have equal objective value. As a result, we put much more effort into avoiding 'losses' than we do to securing 'gains'. For example, if we lose a £10 note in the washing machine, our sadness is likely to be greater than the happiness we feel on finding £10 under a cushion.

In terms of negotiation, this has important consequences in terms of the outcomes people will accept, try to improve through negotiation or just walk away from. While we might like to think that such decisions will be based on a simple question of 'expected value' or 'expected utility' (that is, the net value of each option, or which is 'better'), the perception of outcomes as gains or losses affects how people decide. It can also change the 'neutral' or 'anchor' point from which options are evaluated.

Imagine you are a house purchaser of the type we've been considering.

You are about to offer £100,000 for a house, but an independent third party intervenes. He offers you a choice between one sure option, and another subject to the toss of a coin:

☐ a definite price of £75,000

☐ the possibility of buying it for £50,000 if it's heads, or for your existing offer of £100,000 if it's tails.

Prospect theory tells us that most people would go for the first option, favouring the sure gain over the possible one. Now consider the inverse offer – a choice between:

☐ a definite price of £125,000

☐ the possibility of paying £150,000 if it's heads, or for your existing offer of £100,000 if it's tails.

In this situation, prospect theory suggests that most people would go for the second option; we are happier risking losses than gains.

Fixed pie assumptions

We looked at the difference between distributive ('fixed pie') and integrative negotiations in chapter 2. The term 'fixed pie assumption' refers to the tendency for people to assume or pretend that a negotiation is distributive rather than integrative. In other words, they act on the assumption that whatever is good for the other party must be bad for them. Negotiations usually then close down their focus on a single issue or variable and degenerate into a tug of war or stalemate.

This can be the result of a preference for competitive 'I win, you lose' situations. The desire to compete and win is hard-wired into the psyche. Men are particularly likely to fall prey to the problem, although they do not have the monopoly on it. Social institutions (such as sports) and competitive real-world situations (such as the way promotions are handled within companies) cater to our taste for contests.

There are several negative results of fixed pie assumptions:

- [ ] negotiations aimed at resolving several issues turn into **single-issue negotiations**

- [ ] **win/win outcomes,** options and trade-offs aren't explored

- [ ] negotiators begin trying to **hurt the other party** rather than helping themselves

- [ ] negotiators assume that anything the other side does is aimed at **hurting them,** rather

than furthering a goal, and reject all their proposals

- [ ] negotiators assume that **compromises** are damaging.

The fixed pie assumption is about wilfully ignoring information and options, or failing to see the benefit in them. The keys to fighting it – in yourself and others – are:

- [ ] **share information:** go back over the issues and see if anything important has been missed; explore avenues that might have seemed irrelevant; ask more questions

- [ ] **explore options:** consider carefully what other options might be available

- [ ] **retain a multi-issue focus:** avoid focusing on one issue at a time; bring as many issues into play as possible; consider solutions that address more than one issue

- [ ] **emphasise team play:** get everyone on the same side if possible; discourage any notion of competition or harming the other side.

Read more:

Negotiating Rationally

by Max H. Bazerman and Margaret A. Neale

Escalation of commitment

Difficulties often arise when personal goals become inextricably linked with particular outcomes (the 'fusion' we saw in chapter 3). Once this happens, a negotiator can find it impossible to let go of an outcome without also feeling that they have compromised the goal. In response, they commit themselves more and more strongly to the position, even though such commitment can't be justified on business grounds. This is known as 'non-rational escalation of commitment'.

Any kind of competitive environment is likely to aggravate the tendency for negotiators to escalate commitment. Negotiation becomes a 'trial of strength', or a game of 'chicken', where the test of success is who blinks first.

If commitment escalates on both sides, both negotiators may fall into the fixed pie assumption as well, and adopt the frustration of the other as a desired outcome. They become prepared to 'cut off their nose to spite their face' by accepting an outcome that is damaging to them, as long as it damages the other side as well.

Escalation of commitment is likely when both sides have taken an unreasonable opening position, and consider that they will lose face if they 'back down' from it. Once the opening gambit is made, it cannot easily be withdrawn, however flimsy the basis on which it has been made.

Sunk costs

A sunk cost is a known cost incurred by either party that is somehow linked to the present negotiation, but cannot affect it in any way. For example, in the house-purchase scenario, the buyer might offer a lower price if he becomes aware that the seller bought the house two years ago for £75,000. Her profit in the meantime has no effect on the deal at hand – the only relevant factor is the price for which she will sell. But peripheral facts like these can distort our perceptions, by making us think that past gains on the other side are somehow losses for us, or that they need to be compensated for in the present negotiations.

The 'cost' that is sunk need not be financial. For example, we may be unwilling to walk away from a negotiation because we have 'invested' a lot of time and effort that we don't wish to 'lose'. In fact, taking the present situation at face value, our time and effort are lost whether or not we 'justify' them by reaching an agreement subsequently.

To combat this, financial traders are encouraged to cultivate a 'flat book' mentality: to trade as if they had no history of prior losses and gains. In a similar spirit, they are enjoined to sell any asset that they hold at a price at which they would buy it.

By taking a course of action based on the past, we fall into the trap of 'honouring' sunk costs by orienting actions in the present towards justifying decisions taken in the past.

Other examples include:

☐ continuing to plough through a book we're not enjoying, because of the time we've spent on it

☐ going to a concert even though we're feeling ill, because of the money we spent on the tickets

☐ persisting with a failing product or service because of its R&D cost in the past

☐ retaining a member of staff who isn't performing well because of the effort we have put into training them.

Sunk costs are particularly difficult to work around in negotiation

because we are normally seeking as much additional information as we can to support our position, including precedents. In the course of our research, we may find out information about the past that isn't relevant to the present, but has a strong psychological impact on us. We can't delete it from our memories, so we have to try and disregard it as best we can, or balance it with other information.

Read more :

Judgment in Managerial Decision Making

by Max H. Bazerman

Fairness

As individuals or groups, we can only negotiate from our own perspectives. Negotiation is, first and foremost, about defending our own interests. We are biased towards helping ourselves, however much we recognise the benefit of helping others too. This ego bias can have serious consequences for negotiations, particularly in the area of what is considered 'fair'.

In truth, there is only one 'fair' outcome of a negotiation, which is the one that is acceptable to all parties and realises the most benefit for each of them. However, for most of us, fairness means something far less objective, based on our own preconceptions, beliefs, experiences and cultural background. This can cause problems in negotiation, including:

- **filtering information:** ignoring, minimising or playing down information that does not support your own notion of what is 'fair'

- **uneven commitment:** favouring your own proposed solutions because they are 'fairer'; putting more effort into refining or improving them; withholding effort or support from others' solutions (because they are 'less fair')

- **overconfidence:** assuming that third-party assessments of what is fair will match your own

- **common-good problems:** having difficulty in reconciling mutual and one-sided goals on the basis of what is 'fair for all concerned'.

Setting ground rules for negotiation can help to highlight differences in perception or bring unspoken fairness standards into the open, and establish a genuinely shared sense of what is 'fair'.

Looking back:

Key ideas from this chapter

- Psychological factors have a big impact on negotiation.

- The way we frame negotiations – in terms of information, options, starting positions and opening offers – has a profound impact on how we view outcomes.

- Whether we regard outcomes as 'gains' or 'losses' affects the way in which we compare their value.

- Fixed pie assumptions and escalation of commitment can lead to negotiations becoming aggressive or degenerating into stalemate.

- Our own ideas of what is fair, and the value we place on what we own, can distort our perspectives.

6 Closure:

This chapter looks at overcoming impasses in negotiation, getting commitment to what has been agreed at the end of the process, and the place of negotiation in the wider business context.

Getting back on track

When goals differ widely and a mutually acceptable outcome cannot be found, negotiations can reach an impasse. This isn't always a disaster, nor does it mean that agreement cannot be reached.

We saw in chapter 3 how finding time and space can be useful. The time and space provided by an impasse can allow both sides to think carefully about the situation and what they want from it. As information is revealed and options explored, goals and priorities may change. Those involved may need time to reappraise what outcomes might work for them, and a breakdown in negotiations provides this. However, to realise the benefit, negotiations have to be restarted. The key to this is to re-establish a sense of reasonableness, displacing feelings of mistrust, apprehension or loss of face. Some possible tactics here include:

☐ **revising your goals or desired outcomes,** however slightly, and making this known to the other party (reframing the negotiation)

☐ making a **small concession** to 'kick-start' proceedings

- **calculated altruism:** making a large and unilateral concession in the interests of building trust and cementing the later relationship (this is not as dangerous as it appears: individuals are more likely to reciprocate large acts of generosity than small gestures)

- submitting **information** that puts the negotiation in a new light (the information need not be genuinely new or particularly significant; it merely needs to justify reopening the discussion)

- pretending not to understand that the other side's **walk-outs, inertia or ultimatums** had any significance, and simply arranging another meeting (which allows the other side to re-enter the negotiation without losing face)

- **apologising** for the way negotiations have gone (whether or not you are at fault)

- **changing personnel:** getting new negotiators; appointing mediators (or getting rid of them)

- moving the negotiation away from **audiences** or other external factors that may encourage escalation of commitment.

Managing difference

Management thinkers Warren H. Schmidt and Robert Tannenbaum have identified the management of difference as a key skill in negotiation and conflict resolution.

Differences of opinion are the starting point for negotiation; the process is aimed at resolving such differences to the benefit of both parties. Differences can give rise to negative feelings and strained relationships, particularly when people lack negotiating skills. As a result, people within the business can feel that they have much to lose from differences of opinion; they come to regard them as negative in themselves, when in fact it is only their consequences that are negative.

One of the benefits of learning to be a better negotiator is regarding differences of opinion as productive opportunities for learning, change, innovation or growth. They can challenge complacency within the business by bringing new issues to the surface, and therefore need to be actively managed for business benefit rather than suppressed or ignored. Any negotiation, whether it is between people within the business or those outside it, can offer opportunities for learning; for this potential to be realised, we have to be able to handle differences of opinion in a constructive way.

Managing differences is about looking at the disparity between the two sides in a negotiation: how it originated and how it might be resolved. This means looking at key areas including:

☐ **issues and goals:**

  ☐ are the **issues** that have led to the difference clear?
  ☐ do both parties **agree** about the reason for their difference?
  ☐ are the **goals** on both sides clear? have they been discussed?

☐ **facts:**

  ☐ do both parties have access to the **same information?**
  ☐ do both parties accept that key information is **factual and accurate?**
  ☐ do both parties accept the **authority** of information sources?

☐ **leverage and power:**

  ☐ is there a mismatch in terms of actual or perceived **power?**
  ☐ is there a mismatch between the **leverage** each side feels they have, or that they feel the other side should exercise?

☐ **culture and values:**

  ☐ is there the potential for **cultural differences** to give rise to differences of opinion, or misunderstandings?
  ☐ are there differences in assumptions about **fairness or reciprocity?**

☐ **personal factors:**

  ☐ does the **personal position** of either party affect their perspective?
  ☐ is difference in **negotiation style** a factor?

These questions are particularly useful where a negotiation has broken down and you need to intervene in order to get it started again or mediate between the two parties.

Understanding difference will also form a good starting point whenever efforts at co-operative negotiation seem to have stalled. By re-examining areas of agreement and disagreement, you can focus on how best to move forward again.

Read more:
Management of Differences
by Warren H. Schmidt and Robert Tannenbaum

Reaching agreement

The previous sections of this book have set out how to prepare for the process of negotiation, and some techniques for managing the actual process. Co-operative approaches focus on sharing information and finding an agreement that furthers goals on both sides. Aggressive tactics focus more closely on furthering the goals on one side, with less emphasis on the subsequent relationship. But whatever the style or tone of the discussions, there should come a point where there is an outcome on the table that is acceptable to both parties. It may have been put forward by one side or the other, or worked out through a process of collaboration, but it represents a way forward that both sides are happy with.

Once this outcome has been identified, discussions can move into a more convergent phase, in which practical details can be worked out. It is important to be clear that this phase has been reached, so that both parties understand that they are no longer talking through ideas, but firming up on a chosen option. It may be necessary to go 'back to the drawing board' if practical details turn out to be deal-breakers, but again this reversion should be made explicit. People need to be clear about whether they are throwing ideas around or making concrete commitments for the future.

For your part, you need to return to the preparation stage and ask yourself a few simple questions to ensure that the chosen outcome really is the right one:

☐ does the outcome fully realise the **goals** that you identified before negotiation began?

☐ if there is some **compromise** of your goals in the outcome, what is the trade-off for this?

☐ how far have the **other party's goals** been met? how important has this turned out to be? what will your subsequent relationship be like, given the outcome?

☐ have all the **options** genuinely been explored? is this the best possible deal that could be obtained in the circumstances? if not, what factors outside the scope of the agreement justify accepting a suboptimal deal?

☐ is the outcome genuinely better than your **BATNA**? is there a sense, even at this late stage, in which your BATNA is better than this deal?

- is there any scope for further **improving the deal**, with the proviso that the existing deal can be reverted to if no such improvement can be found (see below)?

- if the deal is of a type that was not foreseen, what are the wider **business implications?** are there potential knock-on effects that could adversely affect the value of this deal to the business?

- has anything **changed** during the negotiation period that puts your goals, or the chosen outcome, in a different light?

- are you sure that the results of the deal are genuinely beneficial in **objective terms** (i.e. not just 'gains' relative to an arbitrarily chosen anchoring point)?

- are you sure that, by reaching this agreement, you are acting for **present benefit** rather than justifying past decisions?

- if you feel a sense of **victory** at the outcome, are you sure that this is because the deal is good for the business, rather than because it vindicates your own commitment or approach?

- is there any sense of wanting to reach agreement because of the **time and effort that have been put into the negotiation,** rather than the benefits of the chosen outcome?

By answering these questions, you can ensure that the deal you are about to commit to is the one you were aiming for at the outset, and also confirm that the way in which negotiations have proceeded hasn't blown you off course.

Getting commitment

Once an outcome has been found that both parties are happy with, an agreement has, in principle, been reached. It's important to take this one step further by securing commitment. This 'seals the deal' by reinforcing it with principles such as consistency and reciprocity. Once this is done, backing down from what has been agreed becomes a transgression or failure.

Ways to fix commitment include:

- **shaking hands** (or corresponding gestures, such as bowing)

- **verbal statements** ('giving your word')

- creating and/or signing **written documents**

- making **announcements**

- agreeing to **penalties** for going back on what has been agreed.

Improving the deal

Once the deal is struck, you will probably feel a sense of relief. But there are circumstances where the story should not end here. The reality is that many negotiations do not reach the best possible outcome. For whatever reason (time pressure, fatigue with the negotiation process, framing effects, etc) we often fail to find the optimum solution from a negotiation.

One option to deal with this is to seek a 'post-settlement settlement' – look at ways in which the deal could be further improved for both parties. If this approach is taken, a crucial proviso is that either party can revert to the initial agreement if they do not like the new version. This is the 'insurance' that makes looking for a 'super-settlement' practically risk-free. It avoids the problems associated with prospect theory, which we looked at in chapter 5, by ensuring that post-deal negotiations can only lead to improvements in the deal, or gains, without any possibility that by continuing to negotiate, either party ends up incurring a loss that they could have avoided. However, such insurance does come with a cost: the potential for wasting time on unrealistic or purely speculative deals that don't offer improvement.

Preparing for the future

Negotiations are about the deals we want to make today, but their focus is usually the future. For example, in recruitments and acquisitions, negotiators make offers and concessions to secure possible benefits at some time in the future, not definite benefits right now. This can cause problems if the parties hold different views of what the future will bring.

In the house-sale example, suppose the buyer has discovered a problem with the property – subsidence in the foundations, perhaps. He might well reduce his offer significantly, perhaps to a point where there is no longer a bargaining zone. He would want to compensate for future problems by paying less in the present. But the seller might not accept that there is a problem, or play down the probability of problems arising.

One answer to the problem is through what is known as a contingent contract – an agreement that part of the deal (probably payment) will be deferred until specific future events have transpired. In the workplace, performance-related pay makes payments contingent on future performance. The fee paid for transferred football players is often made 'dependent on appearances', to avoid argument over whether they will play well and avoid injury in the future.

Contingent deals allow both parties to 'bet' on the outcomes that they think are most likely to happen, so that divergent perspectives on the future can be enshrined in one agreement.

Read more:

Betting on the future: the virtues of contingent contracts

by Max H. Bazerman and James J. Gillespie

Negotiation as a strategic skill

So far we've looked at negotiation as an isolated activity that is aimed at realising specific business goals, such as deciding on prices. Many would say that it is complex enough when considered in this way, but there is also a wider context. In today's business world, negotiation can be a skill of central strategic importance.

Forces such as globalisation, deregulation and new technology are bringing unprecedented and rapid change to business environments. Customers and suppliers have more information and more choice than ever before. To prosper in this environment, businesses need to build robust yet flexible relationships with the companies and individuals who will help them create value. Forging the right kinds of connection takes skills in negotiation, and the business as a whole needs to develop them, rather than leaving it to individuals. Failing to do this results in approaches varying within companies, and valuable learning about negotiation not being shared.

Management writer Danny Ertel suggests four key steps towards making negotiation a corporate capability:

☐ establishing a **company-wide negotiation infrastructure** so that negotiation can be co-ordinated, supported and standardised (where appropriate) like other business functions

☐ **broadening the measures** used to evaluate negotiators' performance from cost to value creation, relationship building, the negotiation process itself and meeting shared goals (and linking these to incentives for improvement)

- drawing a clear distinction between the goals and outcomes of specific deals and the ongoing **relationship** between the parties; teaching the understanding that improvements in one needn't mean that the other deteriorates

- making negotiators feel comfortable when **walking away** from a deal that isn't in the interests of the business; promoting understanding of **BATNAs and leverage**; discouraging any sense of **personal failure** when walking away from a deal.

Negotiators regard themselves – often rightly – as having individual talents that offer big benefits to the business. For this reason, the changes described above need to be introduced with care, to ensure the buy-in of those who will implement them. The key is to generate a new sense of what really brings benefit – moving away from cost savings in specific instances to value for money for the whole business, and towards better relationships across the entire business.

Read more :
Turning Negotiation into a Corporate Capability
by Danny Ertel

Looking back:

Key ideas from this chapter

- Sometimes, negotiations can become stalled and we need to use the right techniques to get them back on track.

- Differences of opinion need to be welcomed and managed to realise opportunities for learning and development.

- Deals need to be sealed with some kind of commitment, written or otherwise.

- It can be helpful to try and improve the deal further after agreement has been reached, or build in conditional aspects that 'insure' against future contingencies.

- Treating negotiation as a skill required at the organisational level can bring real benefits.

Index: